THE SEC
OF SPIRULINA

MEDICAL DISCOVERIES
OF JAPANESE DOCTORS

BioLumina Spirulina
www.newphoenixrising.com
831-704-7369

Edited by

CHRISTOPHER HILLS, PH.D., D.SC.

Japanese edition edited by
DR. NAOHARU FUJII, M.D.

Translated from the Japanese by
DR. ROBERT WARGO
Associate professor of Philosophy and Far Eastern Studies,
Oakland University, Rochester, Mich. USA

Published by University of the Trees Press
in cooperation with
the Journal of Nutritional Microbiology

Printed in the United States
by R.R. Donnelley & Sons
Cover artwork and photography by John Hills

First printing: October, 1980. 40,000 copies
Second printing: June 1981. 100,000 copies

Library of Congress Cataloging in Publication Data

The Secrets of spirulina.

    Includes bibliographical references and index.
    1. Spirulina—Therapeutic use. I. Hills,
Christopher B. [DNLM: 1. Algae—Popular works.
2. Diet therapy—Popular works. WB400 S446]
RM666.S663S4313   615'.32946   80-22087

ISBN 0-916438-38-4 (pbk.)

University of the Trees Press
P.O. Box 644
Boulder Creek, Calif. 95006

Table of Contents

Editor's Introduction to the English Edition   1
Introduction, by the Tokyo Stress Research Society   13

PART I   Spirulina— a food product the world has been   19
                awaiting. Scientists disclose its miraculous properties.

Chapter 1   Nature—the real cure for the diseases of modern man.   19
                Spirulina—a great boon for the Japanese.
                by Dr. Yasusaburo Sugi, Ph.D., M.D.,
                Emeritus Professor of University of Education,
                Department of Physiology, Tokyo

Chapter 2   Why is Spirulina such an astonishing miracle multi-   25
                purpose food? After twelve years of intensive research,
                the essence of Spirulina is finally revealed.
                by Professor Hiroshi Nakamura, Ph.D., D.Sc., Board
                Member (Director), Japan Science Association

PART II   Spirulina's astounding therapeutic efficacy.   55
                Astonishing clinical examples of success with diabetes,
                liver disease and gastroenteric disorders, as reported
                in medical practice by several prominent Japanese
                doctors.

Chapter 3   Remarkable effects on the problem diseases   55
                of our time—diabetes, hepatitis, anemia, etc.
                Spirulina perfect for improving the bodies and
                dispositions of the Japanese people.
                by Dr. Tadaya Takeuchi, Ph.D., M.D.,
                National Medical and Dental University of Tokyo

Chapter 4   Effective in the prevention and treatment of hepatitis   79
and cirrhosis. Spirulina—a way to save and clean the
"medicine pickled" liver of the Japanese people.

*by Dr. Noboru Iijima, Professor at University
Hospital, St. Maryanne College of Medicine*

Chapter 5   Spirulina alone or in food for the treatment   89
of chronic pancreatitis. Ideal food for pancreatitis,
anticipation of its medicinal use.

by Minoru Tanaka, Kyoto Medical College

Chapter 6   Lost vision rapidly restored. Continuous improvement   97
in cases of cataracts, glaucoma, etc.

*by Yoshito Yamazaki, M.D., Lecturer,
Tokyo College of Medicine and Dentistry,
Director, Kazuo Yamazaki Ophthalmic Clinic*

Chapter 7   Amelioration of gastroptosis and ulcers in my patients.   109
Controlling modern diseases of the digestive tract
occasioned by foods with artificial additives.

*by Dr. Tomokichi Sakai, Internist and Physiologist
Professor, University of Eastern Japan*

Chapter 8   A report of success with getting back lost hair   123
(circular depilation) by ingestion of Spirulina.
Only one case, but the depilatory progress was halted
and the downy hair darkened.

*by Dr. Iwao Tanabe, Psychiatrist and Internist (special-
ity in Oriental Medicine) Denen chofu Clinic*

PART III   **Spirulina: a safe food. An account of the**   127
thoroughgoing basic research on its safety.

Chapter 9   Safety and checking is of primary concern in health   127
foods. Pharmaceutical research on the safety of Spirulina.

*by Dr. Kenichi Akatsuka, Ph.D., M.Sc., Professor,
Pharmaceutical University College of Meiji*

Chapter 10   Spirulina safe for hyper-photosensitivity. No possibility   133
of unexpected problems as with Chlorella.

*by Dr. Koji Yamada, Associate Professor,
Koriyama Women's University*

Chapter 11   Spirulina contains no deformity-causing qualities.   139
Reports of complete safety confirmed by animal
experiments.

by Dr. Yoshio Uematsu, Director,
Animal Breeding Research Center

PART IV   **A true health food for the modern age. Spirulina**   147
stands above the ordinary confused "health boom".

Chapter 12   Spirulina an aid for overstressed moderns and their   147
imbalances. Now a food in the true sense, something
between a food product and a medicine.

by Dr. Naoharu Fujii, Director, Tokyo Stress Institute

Chapter 13   Spirulina—the manna of the future.   163
Spirulina—a food resource for an overpopulated world.

by Dr. Hiroshi Watarai, Ph.D., M.D., Director,
Watarai Clinic, Tokyo

Chapter 14   "Green blood" or chlorophyll's positive effects on the   171
entire body. The function of Chlorophyll which
Spirulina contains in abundance.

by Makoto Uno, Science Writer

Chapter 15   Spirulina is a genuine health food. Securing health safety   183
and efficacy in an age of un-"health foods",
proved by several scientists.

by Kasaku Takashima, Medical Journalist

Chapter 16   Eight pictures of Spirulina   196
Two papers on the role of Spirulina's amino acids   197
in metabolism:
          Spirulina, the Maya's Secret
          Spirulina as Nutrition for the Brain   204

by Christopher Hills, Ph.D., D.Sc.

Appendix   How to obtain Spirulina   213

v

DISCLAIMER

WARNING: FDA regulations strictly prohibit the selling of any food product which is represented as a medicine or drug. Therefore, therapeutic claims about the benefits or effects of Spirulina cannot be made in the USA. The editor of the English edition merely presents the medical effects of this Japanese research for the readers to make their own decision. He believes it is not wise to recommend or suggest any medical effects for Spirulina products so as not to obstruct the availability of Spirulina to US consumers as one of the world's most nutritious, well-tested vitamin food supplements.

This disclaimer is made because this book will inevitably be sold in health food stores or wherever nutrition is the uppermost consideration. This book should not therefore be associated with any particular product. The FDA recommends that such literature be placed at least ten feet away from any product that can, by association, mislead a customer to believe that they will be healed or cured by ingesting it. The editor and publisher do not accept any responsibility for the truth of the contents, which are solely the scientific opinion of the authors. They are interested in any and all research into the nutritional effects of microalgae and welcome comments, positive or negative, on the subject matter of this book.

EDITOR'S INTRODUCTION TO THE ENGLISH EDITION

This book of research papers could not have been written in the USA because the laws which govern FDA regulations prevent any products from being used for medical purposes without prior approval. To get approval of a new food or a new drug* requires so much red tape, so many years of mostly animal experiments done according to special rules, that no one in their right mind will develop or apply for approval of a new food or drug unless they are assured of making millions of dollars with it. Even then only large multinational chemical companies can finance the costs of such long experiments. And with a food like Spirulina, a large investment would have to be made in advance to produce the Spirulina in the first place. So there is not much chance of a new food like it ever being developed extensively if it depends on FDA approval. However, because Spirulina is allowed to be sold as a dietary supplement or vitamin product, it should be possible to now duplicate these same experiments here in America. Even so, unless the tests are done under stringent FDA supervision and rules they will not count towards FDA approval of the product. Some governments like the Japanese and Mexican equivalents of the FDA have taken it upon themselves to test it as a food themselves to approve it for their people, because it already has a long history as a food of other cultures past and present, as you will read in the text.

This book is a translation of the work of several Japanese doctors and researchers who decided to subject the microalgae called Spirulina to actual medical tests. In Japan, as in the USA, a vitamin must, in order to be approved, pass a certain number of stringent tests. But even then these tests with animals such as rats and rabbits may not yield results which apply to humans, and so the FDA will not accept tests done in other countries. Consequently, the develop-

---

* It is now estimated that it takes $5 million and 10 years to get a new drug approved, but 5 years ago it took $1 million and 5 years.

ment of any new food or drug is discouraged and the American people are the losers. In Europe and Japan many new developments can take place which are prohibitive and too costly in the USA. This book then is a great blessing because it gives us knowledge which no one would attempt to get in the USA because of the high cost of medical tests. Spirulina is one of those products of nature which should come under what is called the "Grandfather clause", an approval of safe foods eaten for so long by mankind that it would be stupid to ban them merely because they have not been tested by FDA rules. Because the Mexican government saw Spirulina as a new source of high protein and as a great potential resource they asked the United Nations Laboratories to test it and prove its specifications. As this analysis is not in the Japanese book I am including it at the end of my introductory note to the English edition.

I consider it a great privilege to edit this book, as I was with Professor Nakamura when he got so excited about Spirulina in 1967. He had come to Centre House in London where I had just founded an experimental community and he stayed with us a couple of months preparing a Chlorella algae project for India. In his book *Future Foods,* which we are translating right now, he recounts his early experiences with different kinds of natural new food organisms while hunting for the ideal species. No one can conceive of what an enormous job this is, considering that there are over 10,000 different species of algae to choose from. To find any microalgae which already has a long history of being eaten as food, apart from the traditional Japanese seaweed (nori) is very rare, so we should be grateful towards all those microbiologists who had a part in its rediscovery.

In our book *Food From Sunlight* Prof. Nakamura and I outline the early biological knowledge of algae mass culture up to 1965. We had previously met to facilitate a project in 1963 in Utah, where he stayed three months growing Chlorella-inoculation cultures while waiting for the financial partners to raise enough money. I asked him several years later to come again to Kansas in the US for three months to set up an algae farm on a cattle ranch but again the financial courage of the investors was weak. It was not until Dr. Nakamura returned to Japan as a consultant to most of the Japanese algae farms that full production of Chlorella and Spirulina began to take off. At the same time the Mexicans discovered they had a wild species called Spirulina G.J. deToni growing in Lake Texcoco, so that now after 10 years the world production is near to 1,000 tons a year. Now that the technology is known, Spirulina has been widely researched, although there is quite a gap between people who have intellectual knowledge in the laboratory and the actual manifestation of Spirulina in the field on a large scale.

Two or three American companies have attempted to grow Spirulina over the last five years and failed, each of them losing about $600,000. However, the design of these projects was extremely weak and the American experts did not follow any of the Japanese experience of Dr. Nakamura or the Mexican producers, and so they fell on their noses so to speak. There is no reason for failure today except lack of real knowledge.

If conditions are right, Spirulina grows itself, as it does in Mexico, Ethiopia, Lake Chad and certain lakes in Kenya. It grows itself in my test tubes and in 6 gallon bottles in my warehouse where I just leave it in optimum conditions and forget about it. But you cannot do that with a big crop out in the open ponds without risking failure. If you grow it on a large scale by artificial means you must watch over it daily and hourly. It grows so fast, that you only have a few hours to weed a pond if an alien strain of algae decides to take up residence in your ponds. As a retired man I have no wish to babysit little baby Spirulina organisms everyday, so my involvement in American developments has been more as a consultant to those who wish to grow and market it in this country. However, I am vitally interested in finding any natural conditions where I can plant a seed culture and let nature grow it wild and let it multiply. Hot springs and warm spa waters with bicarbonates and lots of sunshine are not only attractive to wealthy humans, but also to my mistress of so many years called Spirulina. It has been a long love affair so I know her tantrums well. Although it grows slowly at 110°, Spirulina likes to grow at the preferred temperature of 95 to 98°, the same as human blood. It may not be without accident that the porphyrin molecule, which is the pyrrole-shaped nucleus of the Chlorophyll structure, is also the same porphyrin nucleus of the hemoglobin molecule of the red cells of human blood. The ideal temperature of the human body may even be stabilized by the control mechanism of the brain at 98.6, because it knows that red blood cells grow best at that ideal temperature of the porphyrin nucleus. This is pure speculation of the author which would have to be tested by experiment in the laboratory, but it is remarkable that these two factors common to both blood and Spirulina are identical. This may also account for Spirulina's rapid assimilation into the human body and its rapid conversion of its amino acids into glycogen in the liver. The energy rush felt by joggers and athletes from eating Spirulina begins to take place almost within minutes of ingesting the powder. When fasting and feeling tired through hard work a teaspoonful of Spirulina is equivalent to an immediate pick-me-up, so perhaps there is more than speculation in the thought that the similar structure of hemoglobin and chlorophyll plays a distinct role in enhanced metabolism in the human body.

Some have questioned why I call it plankton, because they believe that plankton is only small animal life eaten by whales and they get mixed up in their imagination with krill, shrimp and so forth. Although the strict definition of plankton is any vegetable or animal microorganism which drifts with the tides and water currents, it was confused with small animals which swim. Zoo plankton which have means of propulsion are called Nekton. Even though there are some vegetable algae which do have little paddles on them and do swim and are quite active under a microscope, the term plankton is reserved for those cells which forage for their nourishment entirely by drifting passively in a medium. Spirulina is part of that major plant group of algae called phyto-plankton. Therefore calling Spirulina plankton is correct whether it is marine type Spirulina or inland. I call it vegetable plankton because as a food supplement there is so much prejudice in America against the type of algae which people try to eradicate from their swimming pools. Some of the algae types which grow on ponds and pollute rivers are poisonous, even though they take up and absorb pollutants out of the water, thereby purifying it. But if these small plants are not harvested they are soon asphyxiated by their own prolific growth and die. Then they sink to the bottom and pollute the water they have just cleaned up. Thousands of tons of such algae is wasted and allowed to rot when every year it could be skimmed off the lakes and ponds and used as mulch or fertilizer, or even digested in tanks to produce methane. If you see cows sucking a green algae with relish you know it is a favorite type and is nontoxic to animals. You can always feed it to chickens, rabbits, and pigs to find out if it is the toxic kind of algae you have in your local ponds. Algae not only cleans the water by taking up the nitrogen and minerals in it, but the species Spirulina also converts all these normally foul-smelling fertilizers and composts into pure edible vegetable matter. It is a miracle of transformation to see that what are the waste products of one organism are the life support system of another.

Very few humans would eat Spirulina grown on human excreta yet such nutrients would be rendered perfectly chemically safe and pure. A person like Toru Matsui, an 85-year-old philosopher living on Mt. Hakone in Japan, knows this well and has actually fed himself on algae grown exclusively on his own denatured excreta for over 15 years. He intends to continue until the whole world is no longer starving from malnutrition. That is his vow to himself! I have described him in more detail in my other books* on Spirulina.

People's attitudes over the years towards the mass culture of Spirulina have revealed the nature of their beings to me. There are the "Possibility Thinkers" and the "Impossibility Thinkers" who always put me into extreme brackets as a utopian visionary or someone who is hallucinating an end to world poverty and hunger. In fact, most of the people working for world hunger are immersed in so many mounds of facts and figures of impossible corn production and soya beans and wheat reserves, that they have shown little or no interest in the "Possibility Thinkers" who have continually thrust the high proteins of Spirulina under their noses. They looked and they saw and they sniffed and went right on talking about

---

* *Food From Sunlight* $14.95 and *Rejuvenating the Body* $2.50 published by University of the Trees Press.

wheat, water and land, exports, ships and governments. The task of feeding the world is totally beyond them, yet they cannot stop their rationalizing and tune into the vast potential of the world's future food. Enough Spirulina can be grown in the right conditions to feed the entire planet. What is more, Spirulina can be grown right where it is needed so that exports, ships and gasoline transport are not required in its distribution. But the "Impossibility Thinkers" are self-defeated before they start out, so they cannot see or hear anything but the deafening roll of doomsday talk, constantly repeating the worn clichés of the relief agencies.

Spirulina is not just a relief food, it is a complete departure into a new way of farming without any plows, animals or expensive gasoline tractors. It can even be used as raw material to make synthetic fuels, electricity for pumping, and energy for houses. Harvesting can be taught in far less time than it has taken to learn how to grow rice or wheat or soybeans. And for the farmer it is an electric pump that does all the leg work, the preparation of the soil and the harvesting of the crop. Yet the "Impossibility Thinkers" have repeatedly thrown one worn untrue cliché after another on every scheme which has been proposed, to the point that the author does not even bother to go to any of those "feed the world" meetings, film shows and conferences. They are wrestling with the impossible, so they know they are going to lose the battle. Whereas the "Possibility Thinkers" are looking for a cosmic secret in such miracle foods as Spirulina. The daunting fears of human imaginations are irrelevant to those who have discovered the secrets of Spirulina.

The idea of Chlorella as a world food was developed independently by Prof. Hiroshi Nakamura and myself in 1957. When we met it was a case of instant combination of intellects which would daily trigger off ideas for mass photosynthesis growing systems, so that when Spirulina came along it produced immediate excitement. Prof. Nakamura immediately went back to Japan and formed the Japanese Spirulina Development Committee. He recommended the food for feeding fancy carps (koi), because he had been feeding it to his pet angel fish and found their colors changed miraculously golden yellow. In those years we started with the idea that, for feeding the hungry people of the world, a mass refinery-type large installation would get the production quantity big enough to drop the price to 10¢ per pound, so that the poverty stricken countries could afford to buy it. But no one would listen, no government or millionaire would respond. Now that the price is high and Spirulina in the USA is beginning to be a vitamin supplement, everybody is wanting to buy it and millionaires want to invest in it as a venture. Our "Possibility Thinker" realizes that one day we will produce thousands of tons of Spirulina; and then the prices will go cheaper and cheaper until poor hungry people can afford it. But it will probably get more expensive at the beginning—as long as there is a shortage and the cost of small-scale production is high. But even at today's prices it only works out at $1.00 per day because Spirulina is so concentrated and so nutritious that you only need a dollar's worth a day to stay alive. Try to get anyone in the USA or Japan to stay alive for $1.00 a day, or $365.00 a year!

So there is a possibility in the consciousness of people that the humble algae that everyone throws away and kills in their swimming pools may one day feed the world at large. Our local University Community School parents have decided to sell Spirulina to their friends to earn extra wealth for themselves, and to give the school a nonprofit income for running the school at the same time. I never dreamed way back in 1963 that algae would sell to finance our children's education or that it would become the main food of the fancy koi carp, but I never lost my faith in Spirulina. You know why? Spirulina fits the description in Exodus, chapter 16* exactly because its cells double themselves in 24 hours and when there is no nitrogen or ammonia present on the rocks it grows white in color and all its 71% protein turns into polysaccharides and makes it sweet. Algae also stinks and goes rotten in the small pools on the surface of the rocks when you don't harvest it because it dies and the worms and flies love it. The condensation, rain, and morning dew is enough to bring the dormant cells to life again.

---

* Exodus 16: 4, 14, 20, 31.
4 Then said the Lord unto Moses, Behold, I will rain bread from heaven for you; and the people shall go out and gather a certain rate every day, that I may prove them whether they will

Sometimes we can see algae bloom like a hoar frost on the spring soil, like a thin carpet of green, but where there is only rock it may grow white, like a wafer dried in the hot sun. The scoffers and "Impossibility Thinkers" could not offer a better explanation than this.

Well, all I say is try some for a while and you will soon experience why they called it "Manna from Heaven". I visualize somewhere about 300,000 acres of arid desert lands being turned into the food basket of the world. I see the tanks of plastic sheet membranes spread in rows as far as the eyes can see, covered by the deep green of Spirulina. Another Bible prophecy fulfilled!*

Spirulina grows in arid deserts in rock pools in highly alkaline situations where nothing else will grow. When the hot sun heats up the rocks so hot you can't touch them it dries up the alkaline pools on the rocks and leaves the Spirulina dried like a wafer on the rocks. It grows in the desert regions of Ethiopia, Kenya and Chad spontaneously wild. Do you know it even grows in the arid Sinai desert? Do you know what kept my faith in Spirulina when no one would listen? I knew, instantly, when Dr. Nakamura first told me of Spirulina, that it was the food found by Moses which the Israelites discovered was so nutritious that they called it "Manna from Heaven" and they lived on it in the barren desert for years and years. Do you know how many "Impossibility Thinkers" there are who ask me, "How do you really know it was the Biblical 'Manna from Heaven'? You weren't there!"

I have written more extensively about the potentials and uses of Spirulina in other books, but if "Possibility Thinkers" ever run out of possibilities, I could gladly go on and on. But I suspect that they, like me, have got their hands full! The uses of Spirulina are endless. Here, in this book, we are being treated to the specific and exact measured use of Spirulina by scientists, who as doctors may be a lot more conservative than me. They had the courage and the

---

walk in my law, or no.   14   And when the dew that lay was gone up, behold, upon the face of the wilderness there lay a small round thing, as small as the hoar frost on the ground. 20   Notwithstanding they hearkened not unto Moses; but some of them left of it until the morning, and it bred worms, and stank: and Moses was wroth with them.   31   And the house of Israel called the name thereof Manna: and it was like coriander seed, white; and the taste of it was like wafers made with honey.

* Isaiah, chapter 35.

patience to try out the Spirulina with specific diseases and to then document the results. As I said before, the "Impossibility Thinkers" in the USA will not sanction the use of any substance at all for medical reasons without its receiving approval as a new food or drug. So let's keep Spirulina as a nutritional supplement in the USA and let the rest of the world and the Japanese doctors use it to obtain the medical effects of healing. I would counsel no one to use it as a drug in the USA, but you are still entitled to try Spirulina out for yourself as a nutritional supplement or on any of your own ideas concerning good health. If you give it to your dog or cat, they, like the koi carps of Japan, will soon tell you in their own way to give them more and more. Maybe in some things the dumb animals are smarter than man!

I am indebted to the executives of Sosa Texcoco S.A. and Greater Japan Ink and Chemical Co. Ltd. for the color pictures of their production facilities, which do not appear in the Japanese edition of the book. The Mexican company was the first to produce Spirulina on a large scale and is part of a government-owned industrial bank. Sosa Texcoco has stimulated the testing of Spirulina for toxicity and side-effects according to government standards. They have encouraged a former toxicity expert of the United Nations Industrial Development Organization (UNIDO) to complete a two-year study on birth defects in rats and found no problems. Spirulina has been fed for long periods to cows, bulls, chickens, flamingoes, pigs, shrimp, fish and oysters without any side-effects. Long fasts from 30 to 107 days on Spirulina alone have been done by myself and at least 50 of my students without any harmful side-effects.

If we ever see 10¢ per pound Spirulina I shall be the happiest man, but that will be irrelevant because it's better to have the Spirulina available today at a dollar a day than to wait 25 years for 10¢ a pound and not have any.

I get letters every day telling me what Spirulina has done for people medically but I cannot publish them in America because Spirulina would then be considered a drug. Maybe if Americans would eat more Spirulina the bureaucrats who protect us against so many unscrupulous pollutants of foods, will give this pure vegetable a clean bill of health.

Christopher Hills, Ph.D., D.Sc.
University of the Trees, 1980.

Dr. Nakamura and Toru Matsui, a Japanese philosopher who has lived exclusively on microalgae for the last 15 years. They are shown reading a copy of the book *Nuclear Evolution* in 1977.

CHEMICAL ANALYSIS OF SPIRULINA

CHEMICAL COMPOSITION

Moisture	7.0%
Ash	9.0%
Proteins	71.0%
Crude fiber	0.9%
Xanthophylls	1.80 g/kg of product
Carotene	1.90 g/kg of product
Chlorophyll a	7.60 g/kg of product

TOTAL ORGANIC NITROGEN 13.35%

Nitrogen from Proteins	11.36%
Crude Protein (%N x 6.25)	71.0%

ESSENTIAL AMINOACIDS

Isoleucine	4.13%
Leucine	5.80%
Lysine	4.00%
Methionine	2.17%
Phenylalanine	3.95%
Threonine	4.17%
Tryptophan	1.13%
Valine	6.00%

NON-ESSENTIAL AMINOACIDS

Alanine	5.82%
Arginine	5.98%
Aspartic Acid	6.43%
Cystine	0.67%
Glutamic Acid	8.94%
Glycine	3.46%
Histidine	1.08%
Proline	2.97%
Serine	4.00%
Tyrosine	4.60%

VITAMINS

Biotin (H)	average	0.4	mg/kg
Cyanocobalamin (B_{12})	average	2	mg/kg
d-Ca-Pantothenate	average	11	mg/kg
Folic Acid	average	0.5	mg/kg
Inositol	average	350	mg/kg
Nicotinic Acid (PP)	average	118	mg/kg
Pyridoxine (B_6)	average	3	mg/kg
Riboflavine (B_2)	average	40	mg/kg
Thiamine (B_1)	average	55	mg/kg
Tocopherol (E)	average	190	mg/kg

MOISTURE 7.0%
ASH 9.0%

Calcium (Ca)	1,315 mg/kg
Phosphorus (P)	8,942 mg/kg
Iron (Fe)	580 mg/kg
Sodium (Na)	412 mg/kg
Chloride (Cl)	4,400 mg/kg
Magnesium (Mg)	1,915 mg/kg
Manganese (Mn)	25 mg/kg
Zinc (Zn)	39 mg/kg
Potassium (K)	15,400 mg/kg
Others	57,000 mg/kg

STEROLS

	325 mg/kg
Cholesterol	196 mg/kg
Sitosterol	97 mg/kg

Dihidro 7 Cholesterol ⎤	
Cholesten 7 ol 3 ⎬ —	32 mg/kg
Stigmasterol	
others ⎦	

NUTRITIONAL VALUE

Protein Efficiency Ratio (PER) of 2.2 to 2.6 (74-87% that of casein)		
Net Protein Utilization (NPU) of 53 to 61% (85-92% that of casein)		
Digestibility of 83 to 84%		
Available Lysine	average	85%
NITROGEN FROM NUCLEIC ACIDS		1.99%
Ribonucleic Acid (RNA) RNA = N X 2.18		3.50%
Deoxyribonucleic Acid (DNA) DNA = N X 2.63		1.00%

CAROTENOIDS 4,000 mg/kg

α Carotene		traces	
β Carotene	average	1,700	mg/kg
Xanthophylis	average	1,000	mg/kg
Cryptoxanthin	average	556	mg/kg
Echinenone	average	439	mg/kg
Zeaxanthin	average	316	mg/kg
Lutein and Euglenanone	average	289	mg/kg

TOTAL LIPIDS 7.0%

Fatty Acids	5.7%	
Lauric (C_{12})	229	mg/kg
Myristic (C_{14})	644	mg/kg
Palmitic (C_{16})	21,141	mg/kg
Palmitoleic (C_{16})	2,035	mg/kg
Palmitolinoleic (C_{16})	2,565	mg/kg
Heptadecanoic (C_{17})	142	mg/kg
Stearic (C_{18})	353	mg/kg
Oleic (C_{18})	3,009	mg/kg
Linoleic (C_{18})	13,784	mg/kg
γ Linolenic (C_{18})	11,970	mg/kg
α Linolenic (C_{18})	427	mg/kg
Others	699	mg/kg
Insaponifiable	1.3%	
Sterols	325	mg/kg
Titerpen alcohols	800	mg/kg
Carotenoids	4,000	mg/kg
Chlorophyll a	7,600	mg/kg
Others	150	mg/kg
3-4 Benzypyrene	3.6	mg/kg

Toxicology   Nontoxic

Heavy Metals	Typical	
Arsenic (as As_2O_3)		1.10 ppm
Cadmium (Cd)	less than	0.10 ppm
Lead (Pb)		0.40 ppm
Mercury (Hg)		0.24 ppm
Selenium (Se)		0.40 ppm

TOTAL CARBOHYDRATES 16.5%

Ramnose	average	9.0%
Glucane	average	1.5%
Phosphoryled cyclitols	average	2.5%
Glucosamine and muramic acid	average	2.0%
Glycogen	average	0.5%
Sialic acid and others	average	0.5%

TYPICAL MICROBIOLOGICAL ANALYSIS

	SPIRULINA		POWDER MILK	
	MAXIMUM VALUE	MINIMUM VALUE	STANDARDS IN MEXICO	STANDARDS IN USA
Standard Plate Count	20,000/g	4,000/g	50,000/g	50,000/g
Fungi	10/g	3/g	20/g	11/g
Yeasts	10/g	3/g	20/g	11/g
Coliforms	20/g	3/g	20/g	11/g
Salmonella	None	None	None	None
Shigella	None	None	None	None
E. Coli Enteropathogene	None	None	None	None

OTHER TOXICS
Cyanide (CN)   0.20 ppm
PESTICIDES   All negative

α BHC   DDT
1, 2, 3, 4, 5, 6   1, 1, 1 Trichloro-2, 2-bis
Hexachlorocyclohexane Neg.   (p Chlorophenyl) Ethane Neg.

β BHC   op'DDD
1, 2, 3, 4, 5, 6   1, 1 Dichloro 2- (0-Chlorophenyl)
Hexachlorocyclohexane Neg.   Ethane Neg.

γ BHC   pp'DDD
1, 2, 3, 4, 5, 6   1, 1 Dichloro 2- (p-Chlorophenyl)
Hexachlorocyclohexane Neg.   2(p-Chlorophenyl) Ethane Neg.

δ BHC   op'DDE
1, 2, 3, 4, 5, 6   2, 2 bis (p-Chlorophenyl)
Hexachlorocyclohexane Neg.   2-2 p Dichloroethylene Neg.

PHYSICAL PROPERTIES
Appearance: Fine powder
Color: Dark green
Odor and taste: Mild, resembling sea
                     vegetables
Bulk Density: 0.5 g/l
Particle Size: 9-25 microns

Editor's note:

In all laboratory tests of Spirulina and its constituent amino acids there will be differences with each test and each sample, especially because Spirulina is a natural product varying in pigments, proteins, and carbohydrates with the seasons and local conditions. Spirulina can even be made to turn its 71% proteins into 70% polysaccharides by nitrogen starvation and pH change. Each sample will test a little different depending on its source, the type of strain, the nutrients and environment. Such allowances should be noted between Japanese, Ethiopian and Mexican profiles.

INTRODUCTION

by the Tokyo Stress Research Society
(Chartered in Tokyo)

*A safe, effective, natural food for you—Spirulina
—A natural food recommended by Japanese doctors as highly
nutritious, digestible and efficient.*

Spirulina is a name which is not very familiar to most people. It is derived from the Latin word for "spiral". Spirulina is a microalgae plankton vegetable food which is both ancient and new. It has recently been receiving much attention as a health food which has a high nutritive value and has been well tested in Japan for its medical benefits. It has been utilized as an everyday food in both Mexico and Africa since ancient times and with the modernization of the food industry it is today being added daily to foods such as cheese, soup, seaweed (nori), ice cream, chocolate, and grains. In particular the Mexican government in 1973 approved and licensed Spirulina through the equivalent of its FDA as an edible foodstuff after testing it for palatability and toxicity and recommending it for daily use in the home. Moreover, in France, palatability tests are now being conducted along with other efforts to give Spirulina its place in modern food processing.

The geographical places of origin for Spirulina are Mexico and Africa but modern science has only very recently investigated it. When it was studied, nutritive analysis revealed that it contained 69.5% protein, 12.5% complex sugars (carbohydrates), 8% fat, plus many vitamins, amino acids, minerals and food colorations!

Nonetheless, no matter how high the nutritive value of a food, it cannot be called a superior or outstanding food product on that account alone. With respect to this point it should be noted that Spirulina has a soft, thin cellular membrane and is exceedingly digestible. In fact, digestibility tests have shown that its rate of digestion is about 95%. There have been food products made from seaweed before, of course, such as Chlorella, but Chlorella has a hard cell wall and is quite hard to digest; this constituted a barrier to its use as a food source for human beings. But with Spirulina that problem has now been resolved.

Spirulina's safety attested to by scientific authorities

The safety of Spirulina has been thoroughly confirmed by specialists. Based on some reports about Chlorella, the claim has been made that this sort of food, when eaten, would cause dermatitis, and people became quite apprehensive and suspicious. Because of this fear Spirulina was subjected in Japan to the same rigid toxicity tests a medicine would be. The results of these tests fully confirmed its safety.

For details of this testing please refer to the body of the text. There you will find the test reports of scientific workers such as Professor Kenichi Akatsuka, in charge of medicinal substances in the Pharmaceutical Department of the Meiji (University) College of Pharmacology, Assistant Professor Koji Yamada of the Department of Nutrition, Koryama Women's University, and Dr. Yoshio Uematsu, Director of the Animal Husbandry Research Institute.

In Japan there is presently a great deal of criticism being leveled at over-the-counter medicines and drugs sold to the general consumer. The outbreak of side effects resulting from the consumption of medicines in large quantity, for example, the common cold medicine ampules incident, the thalidomide incident, and other incidents of drug poisons have sown the seed of mistrust of medicines on the one hand, and on the other hand there has been a marked increase in the interest of the average consumer in questions of toxicity which, heretofore, concerned only the specialist. It has become a cliché that there is but a hair's breadth of difference between a medicine and a poison, but such uncertainty is surely intolerable in the case of foodstuffs. Nonetheless the existing regulations concerning the production of food products are loose, and this laxity will cause a number of vexing problems to appear in the near future. For this reason Spirulina was checked out and subjected to stringent tests; happily, these tests verified its non-toxicity. In view of all this, it is only natural that it should be sold only as a food for general consumption.

Unfortunately this natural conclusion did not seem so obvious to some. That it was not sold as a natural food must be said to be a defect in the attitudes of the food industry and the food administration in Japan. Basically the main purpose of food is to preserve our health and life. Yet when it comes to the distribution and general sale of foodstuff the major emphasis is apparently placed on an examination of palatibility, which leads to widespread consumption of the product without any assurance of its safety for human health. Here we have a truly frightening situation! Doctors know that too much sugar or salty products may taste nice but are injurious to health. It may be that Spirulina was the first product to be recognized as a thoroughly safe food product in academic journals and yet it has had difficulty in being allowed to take its place in the market place because of its lack of sugar and fears about its palatibility.

Effect on adult geriatric diseases
which modern medicine has difficulty treating

There are a large number of reports attesting to the medicinal effects of Spirulina. In the present volume we have included the reports of leading researchers and clinical specialists in various fields, starting with the report of Dr. Tadaya Takeuchi, Lecturer at Tokyo College of Dentistry, on the effects of Spirulina in clinical situations.

There have been many astounding advances in modern medicine. Because of this the average life expectancy of the Japanese people has been greatly increased, as has their material prosperity. At the same time, however, there has been a dramatic increase in the number of people who complain of physical and emotional disorders and a proliferation of people who have had to suffer from their adult diseases becoming chronic. These "adult diseases" include high blood pressure, diabetes, chronic hepatitis and others like them. They seem to be diseases which even the power of modern medicine can do very little to relieve. If one can speak of "leftovers" with respect to illnesses, it would be in just the case of these illnesses that the term "leftovers" or "oversights" would be most applicable. In particular there are 700,000 victims every year of diseases of the liver in Japan alone and each year 16,000 of these develop cirrhosis of the liver and die. This makes this illness second only to heart disease as a cause of death, and if the situation is not rectified and is left alone it will become the national disease. This is due to the fact that there is no universally agreed upon method of medical treatment. The same is true of diabetes. There just doesn't seem to be any definite way of getting a handle on it.

Patients who suffer from these diseases have no vitality, lose their incentive for work, tire easily and more or less retire from society to sit around home and do nothing in a depressed and lethargic state. Yet a great number of these people have been saved by Spirulina. Of course Spirulina is not a panacea by itself but must be used under the strict supervision of a physician in conjunction with medicine prescribed by him. From the physician's viewpoint it is a supplementary food which compliments and enhances the effects of the treatment prescribed. For example, in the case of diabetes, large amounts of Spirulina are given in conjunction with a strict diet, and the same is true for patients with eye diseases. The treatment requires a strict regimen and lifestyle which includes refraining from between-meal-snacks and eating a balanced diet.

Thus it is that the treatment of modern adult diseases cannot be accomplished effectively without cooperation between the doctor, the patient and his family. Unfortunately there is no special medicine which can effect a cure of these diseases with a simple injection or by taking shots of any drug presently known to medical science.

Spirulina—the offspring of nature and science

In Japan the natural environment is being destroyed and all over the world contaminated substances injurious to human health are being added to food products. It goes without saying that it is important to return the environment to its natural pristine form, but this is not nearly enough. We must progress beyond this to study the relationship between nature and health and go on to select those elements which are beneficial to human health and then utilize these daily in an effective manner. Is this not the essence of human wisdom and scientific progress?

Spirulina is indeed a food which fits the requirements of such a program, for it is a food which was produced naturally, and then through the power of science, using sunlight, air and water, it was cultivated by human artifice. Thus it is a true child of nature and science.

However, in the marketplace today there is already a flood of food products labelled "health food" or "natural food", as well as a growing fad for the "So and So Health Method" or the "Thus and So Treatment." Such a state of affairs bespeaks a frantic, headlong rush for health, and indicates the degree to which interest in, and anxiety about, health has taken possession of the man in the street. But health cannot be attained merely by jumping on a bandwagon. Health can be achieved only by a concerted effort on the part of the individual himself in all aspects and habits of his daily life. We are convinced that Spirulina is a food which can positively contribute to the development of good health in such a sensible daily regimen.

If this volume can be of some assistance in introducing you, the reader, to Spirulina and to an understanding of the role it can play in the promotion of good health, we would consider our efforts to have met with success.

February 1980   The Tokyo Stress Research Society

Spirulina means "little spiral" but few know that Spirulina from Mexico is grown in a big spiral solar farm 2 miles wide which was designed along the lines of the winding shell.

PART I

SPIRULINA—A FOOD PRODUCT THE WORLD HAS BEEN AWAITING
Scientists Disclose Its Miraculous Properties

Chapter One

NATURE—THE REAL CURE FOR THE DISEASES OF MODERN MAN
Spirulina—A Great Boon for the Japanese

by
Dr. Yasusaburo Sugi, Ph.D., M.D.
Emeritus Professor of
University of Education
Department of Physiology, Tokyo

"Nature itself is the best physician"—Hippocrates

Living things, whether they be animal or vegetable, grow strong and healthy in the total natural environment of sun, air, water, and soil while those grown in enclosures such as greenhouses or houses tend to be feeble and weak. Human beings also maintain their health in the context of this same natural environment.

In ancient Greece, the great physician Hippocrates explained the disposition and management of health and disease in accordance with nature and nature's curative powers, concluding that, "Nature itself is the best physician," and that through its adaptive power, "Nature cures while the physician merely assists."

His treatises, *The Sun and Earth, Water and Air,* were, for more than two millenia, until a century ago, regarded as the Bible of medicine which all prospective doctors had to master. At the beginning of his work there is the following passage:

> "What relations are there between the natural environment and the food, drink and very life of the human being? What influence does the environment have over the health and illnesses of each person? We must know the answers to these questions; we must strive to come to understand this." (Ancient Medicine)

The quality of sunlight is reduced in contemporary Japan

However, today with the rapid advance of industrialization a number of momentous problems have arisen due to the progressive pollution of the land, water, and air as well as the blocking out of the sun's rays. This has resulted in calamitous changes in the ecology, deterioration of human health, and the occurrence of disease. In Japan also, since the initiation in 1960 of the governmental policy of doubling the GNP in a decade, the consumption of oil and carbon products has increased precipitously as has the air pollution from automobiles and factories, as well as the deterioration of water quality because of contamination by detergents and industrial waste.

With the air we breathe and the water we drink going bad in this way it is no surprise that our health is affected. Even though the Japanese "Minamata disease" and the "Itai itai Syndrome" may be regarded as extraordinary or "special" cases, it remains a fact that this environmental deterioration commonly induces asthma, allergies, and injury to the respiratory system and the lungs, together with a variety of chronic adult disorders and illness of the whole body.

The same considerations apply in the case of the sun. With the pollution of the atmosphere, the increase in smog, sulfurous acid gas (sulfur dioxide), oxidants and the like, the ultraviolet and Dorno rays which are necessary to human health are to a large extent filtered out of the sunlight which reaches the earth, causing a dramatic decrease in the quality of the sunlight. Herein lies the truth of the saying, "Where the sun does not come, there comes the physician." "Dove non va il sole, va il medico"—Italian Proverb.

When the sunlight is impaired vegetation is deficient and does not grow properly and the health of animals suffer. When human beings eat these deficient plants and animals their health is naturally adversely affected.

The nutritional value of plants and animals is the source of animal energy and the basis of human existence

The appearance of life (DNA) on the earth has been calculated to be about 3 billion years ago. In the beginning the atmosphere was primarily hydrogen and the primitive life forms formed the amino acids, nurtured themselves and lived through enzyme reactions, but in response to oxygen and carbon gases becoming more abundant in the atmosphere the process of photosynthesis became prominent, allowing these life forms to nourish themselves more efficiently (Photosynthesis is over twenty times more efficient than enzyme reactions).

This process of photosynthesis involves the production of nutritive material (protein, carbohydrates, fats, vitamins and others) from carbon gases and water, and one item most essential to this process is chlorophyll, the green pigment in grass and trees. In the process of evolution those forms which possessed chlorophyll became the plants and the animals were those forms that ingested the nutritive materials produced by the chlorophyll of these plants. Thus has the development of animal life continued to this day.

Human beings, as animals, must use plants and other animals as a food source; that is, they depend for nutrition on the nutritive materials produced by chlorophyll either directly by ingesting the vegetable matter itself, or indirectly through the protein bodies of the animals. Moreover, the reason why vegetable matter is essential as part of the animal diet is that in addition to containing protein, carbohydrates and fats (the three major nutritive substances) it also contains large quantities of vitamins, minerals and fibers. In addition the green material of plants (chlorophyll molecules) have the porphyrin nucleus which is also the immediate raw material of the red color of animal blood (hemoglobin). This is the reason that chlorophyll is referred to as "green blood".

The maintenance of health in a civilized society comes from "natural food products"

The pollution of the natural environment and the loss of green pigments continues to pose a great threat to plants, animals and thus to human life. The uneasiness about the world's food supply grows continually more serious, especially with the increase in the world's population. The problem is more one of a steady deterioration of the quality of the food supply than simply a question of the amount, since the lowered quality results in adverse affects on health and an increase in disease.

In order to protect ourselves against this it is crucially important to first obtain good quality food, i.e. natural foods, and to do this we must prevent the further pollution of the atmosphere, water supply and soil and preserve both the natural sunlight and the green vegetation. But in a modern society, with its propensity for urbanization and industrialization, merely raising a hue and cry will not be enough to protect these natural resources.

In this connection we have to realize that although natural foods are said to be those vegetables and grains which are grown without the use of artificial fertilizers and pesticides, these "natural foods" can't function as foods which are conducive to health unless the soil in which they are grown is itself "natural." This is the reason that in America health foods are referred to as "whole earth foods" and why a special group has been formed to carry this message to the general population.

In her book *The Silent Spring* Rachel Carson argues that, because of the destruction of the natural balance of the soil through agriculture and chemical fertilizers, there will come a time when the insects which live in the soil and the birds which are thus dependent on it for their food supply will face extinction. When this happens spring will come but the birds will not sing, the insects will make none of their characteristic sounds and in the end human beings will no longer be able to make their abode there. With images of poetic quality and feeling she proclaims the threat to the existence of life on this planet. This will come when the ecological system is destroyed and we no longer have nature or anything natural left!

The appearance of Spirulina brings hope for a solution

The earth's soil is alive and its condition is intimately bound up with that of the air, water and sunlight. The green vegetables which are grown in that soil are an important source of trace elements necessary to complete nutrition, such as iron, copper, cobalt, manganese, zinc, and important nutrients like potassium, calcium and vitamins. The kernels and shells of grains are the source of elements essential to health, such as the B vitamins and vitamin E. All of these have been shown to be essential to the human diet together with protein, carbohydrates and fats. There is a growing tendency for many of these trace elements which contain these vitamins to be lost or destroyed because of the deterioration of the soil as well as the nature of the manufacturing and distribution processes. The naturalness of food has been one of the most tragic victims of the destruction of the natural environment. This is particularly important to the Japanese since they are basically "herbiverous" and with a decrease in the consumption of yellow and green vegetables as well as vegetative matter from the sea, there has been a poisoning of our metabolic system by fatty food and meat in the European style. With this damage in diet there has been a rising incidence of nutritional imbalance and disturbance of the metabolism which has consequently led to a lowering of the general level of health and the outbreak of "adult diseases."

It is provident at this point in time that Spirulina should have come on the scene as a "true food nutritional supplement" and it must be considered an almost miraculous boon for us now that real natural foods are scarce. Spirulina deserves to be called a true "natural food" because, being rich in chlorophyll and having its special cultivation techniques scientifically confirmed and certified by authorities, we can be assured that its nutritive elements preserve a proper balance. It can be produced safely and with stability under truly natural conditions of air, water and sun. Scientists have great hope for it as a prominent source of vegetable protein in the future and I believe it represents a health food which is desperately needed now by the Japanese and all other people.

Chapter Two

WHY IS SPIRULINA
SUCH AN ASTONISHING MIRACLE
MULTI-PURPOSE FOOD?
*After twelve years of intensive research, the
essence of Spirulina is finally revealed.*

by
Prof. Hiroshi Nakamura, Ph.D., D.Sc.
Board Member (Director), Japan Science Association

The extraordinary excitement produced by my encounter with Spirulina

If one were to suddenly ask most Japanese, "Do you know about Spirulina?" one would most likely get, in response, hesitation and a sucking in of breath, since the word is one with which most are not familiar. Spirulina is a form of algae produced since ancient times in Africa, Mexico and other places which the natives of these areas have consumed as part of their daily diet for many thousands of years. In spite of this history, it was only introduced to modern industrialized societies a scant twelve years ago, and it is small wonder that the average person has not heard of it.

The term "spirulina" is cognate to the English term "spiral," both of which derive from the Latin term meaning twisted or helix form. If one were to translate this term into "pure" Japanese it would be *rasenmo* (spiral alga). Be that as it may, let us now turn to the substance itself to clarify what sort of algae Spirulina is.

In the fall of 1967 I was residing in London at the residence of Dr. Christopher Hills, and it was then I first came in contact with Spirulina. I was surprised by an article which appeared in the topics column of the evening "New Statesman" entitled, "Microorganisms a la Carte." The gist of the article follows:

"In Fort-Lamy, Chad, a country deep in the Sahara Desert, they sell a confection of dark black color called "dihe" in the local language. This confection is made from algae and takes the form of a bun. The native women use a straw basket to scoop the algae, which is the basic constituent of the confection, from the surface of the water of the swamp.

"The amount of protein this algae contains is extraordinarily high, and is a superb food in terms of its nutritional value. It is a new food which bears watching in the future. (It should be given careful scrutiny as a future food source.)

This fantastic spiral solar farming system is two miles across. It is called a "caracol" after the Spanish word for a snail or winding shell or a spiral staircase. The pumps at the center concentrate the brines as they evaporate the waters moving towards the center. To stand at the center is awe-inspiring, knowing that Spirulina, meaning "a little spiral", is growing in this huge spiral solar farm. From the brines the Sosa Texcoco factory makes 650 tons of caustic soda per day and grows four tons per day of Spirulina. For some years the company has subsidized the production of Spirulina to encourage consumption. Recently, export prices in Mexico have been leveled off with the Japanese costs of production.

The cell structure of Spirulina microalgae as seen through a microscope showing the spiral nature of this vegetable plankton which grows into filaments. The cells can be tightly wound in spirals or open as in the above picture.

The cultures are stored in 6 gallon bottles and fed with nutrients and CO_2. Picture shows part of the 75 bottles at the editor's laboratory containing Spirulina, Anabaena and Chlorella cultures which are sold to algae farms for growing seed cultures.

In Japan and Taiwan the seed cultures are grown intensively in flasks before putting out into bigger tanks indoors, prior to seeding the main ponds outdoors.

The editor, Dr. Christopher Hills, at the banquet to launch *The Secrets of Spirulina* in Tokyo with the fifteen Japanese authors and Dr. Fujii, M.D., the editor of the Japanese edition.

The editor, giving a speech at the Tokyo banquet for the authors of *The Secrets of Spirulina* with Dr. Hiroshi Nakamura at his right.

The banquet host for the fifteen authors was DIC who produced the Spirulina used in these tests. DIC is also the world's second largest customer of Sosa Texcoco in Mexico and produces 100 tons of Spirulina a year in its own factory in Siam. The authors are shown with Dr. Fujii, M.D., and Mr. Takemitsu Takahashi, Executive Director of DIC and Mr. Akira Kaneko, Chief of Biochemicals Division of DIC (standing) at the head of the table.

In Taiwan the seed culture from the flasks is placed in the spiral culturing tank indoors until it reaches a rich, deep green color. Paddles aerate and move the water along the stream while CO_2 is bubbled through the growing medium.

The similar type of seed culture tanks outdoors at the factory of Asahi Carbon Co. in Okinawa being examined by a visiting executive of Sosa Texcoco from Mexico.

The seed culture is placed in the outdoor ponds. As far as the eye can see these tanks spiral along the continuous stream system aided by paddles until the algae reaches harvesting stage after two weeks.

In Taiwan and Japan we can see the circular method of growing with the air containing the mix of CO_2 pumped out through small jets in a radial arm which moves around in a circular rotating sweep. This pond is about 1½ feet deep.

Another large algae farm system in Taiwan uses a similar series of round ponds about 148 feet across. The ponds are shallow so that sunlight can penetrate to the bottom.

A close-up of the tanks above showing the radial arm and its jets which aerate the culture. This system can be used for either Chlorella or Spirulina by changing the percentage of the air/CO_2 ratio from 80%-20% for Chlorella to 90%-10% for Spirulina.

The Siam Algae Co., Ltd., is a subsidiary of Greater Japan Ink and Chemicals, Inc. (DIC) in Japan. It commenced operation in October 1978. Siam was chosen after a long search for the ideal climate. DIC manufactures a health food line called Linagreen and Hi-Liena, a food coloring, Lina-Blue and fish feeds for fancy koi (carps). The system of ponds is different from the spiral stream system. DIC produces about 100 tons per year but is also the second largest customer in the world of Sosa Texcoco S.A. in Mexico. The Siam factory uses the Ethiopian strain developed by Professor Nakamura.

A view over the Sosa Texcoco soda plant looking toward the spiral caracol ponds. The white mountain of carbonates in the background are residues of calcium carbonate from the separation of the soda from the brines. Spirulina was a nuisance in their ponds until their executives discovered they had a natural asset and began to harvest it with modern engineering techniques. Today they are the largest producers in the world and will step up production capacity in 1981 to 1000 tons a year.

The Sosa Texcoco S.A. is a government-owned subsidiary of Banco Mexicana Somex, the third largest government bank in Mexico. Their head office building in Mexico City, shown in the picture, houses the offices of many associated companies involved in the production of Chlorine—230,000 tons per annum, 255,000 tons per annum of caustic soda, and 40,000 tons per annum of polystyrene resins. The company maintains the largest aquaculture solar farm system and evaporator in the world at an altitude of two miles (over 10,000 feet) where the natural radiation from the sun is the second highest in the world.

The shallow Lake Texcoco caracol ponds. An employee wades among the filamentous Spirulina algae to examine the quality and take samples of the crop before harvesting. These vast spiral solar ponds, shown in an earlier photograph from a helicopter view, are the equivalent of a gigantic solar energy machine for trapping the energy of light from the sun. This huge natural evaporating machine lifts about 50,000 cubic meters of water a day. The energy required to do this, if it were run by an electric power station instead of the sun, would total 2,200 megawatts.

After being filtered from the concentrated brines the algae is immediately dried in hot air. The large spray dryer is three stories high and dries the algae in hot air of 200° C, but the algae itself never gets higher than 70°C, much lower than temperatures it withstands on desert rocks. At the urging of the editor the Mexican company has agreed to install another dryer and increase production by 100%. It has been agreed to form a new company Aquacultura Nutricional de Mexico S.A. (ANDEMEX) to market tablets and vitamin mixtures for consumption in the Mexican markets. About 150 tons a year will be sold to the Mexico City school district for incorporation into the diets of school children with the approval of the Mexican FDA.

A view towards the soda factory showing the road and the circular pond from the center of the solar farming system. The road is over 2 miles long and capable of supporting heavy trucks, pumping machinery and pipelines. The size of the solar farm is awe-inspiring. It is capable of growing 10,000 to 100,000 tons of Spirulina, the only limiting factor being the harvesting machinery and drying equipment. This photo, taken by the editor, shows a small section of the solar evaporator from the center of the farming system.

The spiral solar evaporation farm concentrates the brines in which the Spirulina is grown. Towards the middle of the spiral caracol pond the algae grows concentrated at a high pH of 9-11 and then dies off. It is harvested while in the deep blue-green stage.

Ing. Durand-Chastell, the first director of Sosa Texcoco to develop the solar ponds for Spirulina, is viewing the culture ponds with an expert from the United Nations. The seed culture is sown in the larger spiral ponds from this area. The United Nations has taken a special interest in developing this extraordinary source of proteins and nutrition as a model for feeding the world from the hundreds of alkaline lakes that abound in Kenya, Australia, Ethiopia and elsewhere. Present high prices and shortage of supply will stimulate production of Spirulina all over the world.

The editor jogging with students. Every day at 5:40 a.m. they meet to jog before beginning work and meditation at 7:00 a.m. Many students have undertaken 30-day fasts on Spirulina and felt more energy on three teaspoonfuls a day than on regular meals. One student fasted for 107 days on three teaspoonfuls a day and signed an affidavit saying that his energy level was more than usual. Marathon runner Frank Aguirre (on left of picture) said that he had more energy after using Spirulina than at any other time of training. A Mexican Olympic athlete has been using Spirulina for five years and won a gold medal in Montreal. Weight lifters and body builders have begun to use it and the current Mr. Mexico has decided to devote his life to introducing Spirulina to the Mexican people.

"According to Belgian and French microbiologists this algae is called Spirulina because of the spiral shape it has. It is usually found in the salt lakes of Africa. This algae is found in salt lakes which have a high concentration of salt. It grows in a strongly alkaline environment. The French National Petroleum Research Center has taken an interest in this algae and is presently planning ways to cultivate it artificially.

"In comparison with Chlorella, Spirulina has a very high protein content. In fact over seventy percent of its dry weight is high-quality protein.

"The International Conference on Applied Microbiology was held here in Addis Abbaba last week (Nov. 10, 1967) and Spirulina was a favorite topic of discussion. The chairman of the conference, Professor Heyden of Sweden, said, 'Because of its high protein content Spirulina must be considered as a future food source.'

"Spirulina also grows wild in the salt lakes of Ethiopia, and since the participants of the conference showed such an interest in Spirulina they set off on a journey to Lake Aranguadi, which is located not far from Addis Abbaba, in order to observe this algae. In this lake Spirulina grows in almost a pristine state, so luxuriantly in fact that the lake seems to be painted over with a deep green paint. Because of its exceedingly high protein content Spirulina certainly deserves to be studied for future use as animal feed and food for human beings also."

Since I myself specialize in microbiology, I read this newspaper article over and over again. I still remember the strange excitement which came over me.

An ideal realized—
large-scale algae with high protein content

There were basically two reasons why this article, which treated Spirulina as an object of scientific inquiry, stimulated my interest. The first reason was that the natives scooped it up with woven straw baskets. If they could scoop it up with straw baskets then it must be a rather large form of algae! If so, this was the very ideal type of algae which scientists had long dreamed of finding.

The other point which excited my interest was the crucial fact that Spirulina's protein content was higher than that of Chlorella. Considering these two points I began to think that Spirulina might just be that ideal food source for the world of the future and that we had better research it thoroughly.*

I had known of Spirulina previously but my acquaintance with it had been limited to reading that it was a type of algae. I never dreamed that it would take this large a form.

When I discovered that it might exist naturally in this large a form I felt my scientific enthusiasm inflamed to the point where, as strange as it may seem to say this, I felt as if I were being drawn to Spirulina by some irresistible force.

When I came to my senses twelve years had passed, years which encompassed a number of memorable experiences and hard work in researching this substance. Sometimes it seemed as if I were running a race all by myself, and when I look back to see who there was following me I would find no one there. I had this feeling of loneliness and isolation many times.

---

*Editors Note: Dr. Nakamura, along with the editor, was the original founder of the Chlorella International Union, whose headquarters was at Centre House in London from 1965. It was at Dr. Nakamura's urging that the name of this organization was changed to Microalgae International Union because of the discovery of Spirulina Microalgae as a feasible world food of the future. It was subsequently discovered growing wild in Lake Texcoco in Mexico. Since then factories have been established in Thailand, Okinawa and Taiwan using Dr. Nakamura's methods.

Happily, however, this was not to continue, for one after another new researchers in the field began to appear on the scene and one by one the constituents of Spirulina began to yield to analysis. Japan's research in Spirulina started rather late compared to other countries but now has more than equalled the world level with the results of the Japanese research being published in technical and scientific journals and receiving much respect.

What this comes to is that vegetable Spirulina, an alga, is a plant which deserves to be the object of scientific scrutiny. There are still many things about Spirulina which we do not yet understand and the real research work, the real results of exact knowledge, have yet to be completed. In most universities it is still numbered among the unknowns of the plant world and that is precisely why it stands as a challenge to the research scientists of the world. Thus, what I am about to relate is only what we know so far, just a small part of the whole, so please read the piece in that light.

In Chad, Spirulina is even now the staple food

Spirulina was first discovered, brought to the world's attention and given a scientific name in 1827 by a German algae specialist named Deurben. As the above article from the "New Statesman" stated, Spirulina is even now a regular part of the normal daily diet of the inhabitants of Chad. Chad is a republic (formerly a dependency of France) in the depths of the Sahara Desert which contains a large lake called Lake Chad. Part of that lake has a separate name and is called Lake Johann where Spirulina grows naturally in profusion.

Lake Johann has a very high salt concentration, so high that there are no fish or shell species living in its waters. Moreover, since it is a desert region which is not suitable for most animal life, the Spirulina which naturally grows in such abundance on the surface of the lake is the only source of protein for the inhabitants of the region.

The method of harvesting the Spirulina is to scoop it up in baskets woven of straw, pour it out on the sand to drain, and then dry the algae in the sun. After this, it is ground into powder and stored. For use as food, the Spirulina is mixed with wheat and baked into a bread or drunk as a soup with spices added. It is even made into a confection which has the appearance of small buns.

Thus for the natives of the area around Lake Chad, Spirulina has been a familiar staple food for thousands of years and constitutes an indispensible source of protein.

Spirulina—a daily food of the Aztecs

There are also records and recently discovered historical evidence indicating that Spirulina was part of the ordinary diet of the Aztecs of Mexico. The Aztecs, who used it as a daily food, were a tribe of Indians living in the high plains of ancient Mexico. In these plains, 2,000 meters above sea level, there are a number of lakes with high concentrations of salt and many intricate Mayan waterways in which they grew Spirulina as a crop in South Mexico. Lake Totalcingo to the south of Mexico City and Lake Texcoco to the north are said to be two of these lakes. These lakes contain vestiges of the same culture to this very day.

Columbus' discovery of the Americas in 1492 was a prelude to rapid European expansion, including the Spanish invasion of Mexico. Cortez and his conquistadors subjugated the Aztec Empire which flourished in the high plains in 1525. After conquering the land and people of Mexico the Spaniards systematically filled in these lakes in the high plains to obtain more farm land. Lake Texcoco, which was left over from this project, is now an extensive marshland with a shallow man-made part of the lake turned into a spiral.

Lake Texcoco is a salt lake rich in soda (sodium carbonate) to the extent that a company, Sosa Texcoco, was formed in 1943 to produce the soda commercially. The Texcoco Company has now drilled about 300 wells in the marshland to extract salt water from a depth of eighty meters. The salt water is then put in a spiral evaporation bed constructed as a pond for this purpose so that the action of the sun's rays will increase the concentration. The concentrated salt water is then pumped to a large chemical factory.

A picture of the spray-drying equipment, showing the Spirulina plankton taken straight from the ponds, harvested fresh and packed into drums.

Commercial production of Spirulina plankton underway in Mexico.

A view of the extensive growing and harvesting ponds showing the Spirulina in its final stages of production.

Nutritional Analysis		Essential Amino Acids	
Protein	71%	Lysine	4.71%
Fatty acids	5.57%	Phenylalinine	4%
Fibre	1.53%	Leucine	5.8%
Carbohydrate	13%	Iso-Leucine	7.28%
Minerals (ash)	9%	Methionine	2.17%
Moisture	7%	Valine	7.71%
Chlorophyll	76mg%	Threonine	5.15%
Calories per tablet	1.97	Tryptophane	1.13%

For comparison 8 grams of Spirulina contains approximately the same vitamins, proteins and amino acids as 100 grams of Tofu. Spirulina is probably the world's highest source of B_{12}.

Vitamin	(mg. %)	(†)	Vitamin	(mg. %)	(†)
A	8000 IUS	170%	Pant. Acid	1.10 mg	10%
B_1	5.50 mg	10%	Iron	5.80 mg	28%
B_2	0.04 mg	8%	Niacin	1.18 mg	2%
B_6	0.50 mg	20%	Calcium	1 315 mg	1%
B_{12}	0.20 mg	100%	Zinc	3.90 mg	25%
E	1.90 mg	8%	Phos.	89.42 mg	2%
Folic Acid	0.50 mg	50%	Mag.	19.15 mg	2%

† Percentage of US RDA per 6 tablets

The pond where the salt water is stored for concentration is a vast Caracol Pond which measures three kilometers and so is quite extensive.

This pond is rather shallow (only fifty centimeters deep) but the salt water which comes up from the bottom is not considerable. Thus on the perimeter of Caracol Pond there is constructed an extra canal of 150 meters which functions as a reserve pond into which is poured river water with high concentrations of salt.

However, the surfaces of both Caracol Pond and the Reserve Pond came to be covered with extensive and luxuriant algae growth. The water in the reserve pond was particularly favored in this respect, much to the surprise of the Texcoco Company officials. In fact this algae was Spirulina, which had grown naturally from Aztec times in the marshland. That it should have grown so luxuriantly in this artificial environment seemed to indicate that, serendipitously, the proper conditions for cultivating Spirulina artificially had been discovered.

Thus it is that the Caracol Pond has come to be thought of the world over as the place where Spirulina grows spontaneously. The one to have reaped the benefit of this providential stroke of luck was the Texcoco Company which has gained a new by-product, Spirulina, in the process of producing thousands of tons of soda which was their main concern. They now harvest one or two tons of the Spirulina each day, much of which is exported to Japan as animal feed and for feeding Koi (fancy carp).

Careful cultivation of the best pure strains using the most modern facilities selecting the best from the thirty-five strains of Spirulina

France was the first country in the world to capitalize on the abundant nutritional elements in Spirulina and envision the mass production of it as a synthetic food product in 1963. Professor Clement of the French National Oil Research Institute (Institute Francais de Petrol) led the way, and this resulted in the industrialization of the Chad Spirulina (producing a mother strain).

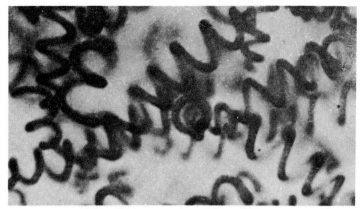

Cell structure of Spirulina as seen through a microscope, showing spiral nature of the vegetable plankton.

Japanese packaging of a Spirulina product for the fast growing of competition fish—used by fish fanciers to improve color and vigor.

In Japan our research on Spirulina began in earnest in 1968. A project team was gathered together to make a start towards industrialization with the assistance of Dr. Christopher Hills of the London-based Microalgae International Union. After 2 years our research was taken over by the Dainippon Ink Kagakukogyo Kabushikikaisha (Greater Japan Chemical Ink Industries Inc.— hereafter referred to as DIC) who succeeded in mass producing Spirulina. Their product was of high quality and was very well received.

Although the time frame was seven years behind that of France, the research in Japan was of an independent nature and the strain used was one from Ethiopia rather than Chad. Why was an Ethiopian strain used in the research in Japan? This is precisely the question I should like to answer in some detail in this article from the viewpoint of one who was involved in the original development of this project.

One speaks of Spirulina as though it were simply one kind of algae, but in fact there are 35 strains of algae that belong to the botanical classification, Spirulina. Among these are some which are not at all suitable for use as a food and some which have low nutritional value. Thus, our first task was to select an appropriate strain to develop, to find the one most likely to fulfill all our requirements for human consumption. To that end we developed a list of standards/requirements and decided to concentrate on that strain which got the highest overall score.

The adaptability criteria were: 1) absolutely no toxicity; 2) high nutritional value; 3) high fertility; and 4) ease of harvesting. All four were considered necessary requirements and any strain which failed to meet any one of these criteria would be dropped from consideration. This was intended to be a very stringent test of candidates.

If one may be allowed to make the analogy with university science examinations, our first test was the written exam. That is to say, we thoroughly examined all the existing world literature on lakes and swamps. From the basic survey that had been done already we knew that Spirulina grew spontaneously in a natural state in the salt lakes of tropical climates where the concentration of salt was quite high. Accordingly we collected and studied the literature on limnology. The cooperation of a large number of researchers went into this survey of documents and the result was that strains of Spirulina which would be likely candidates were known to grow naturally in the following eight lakes:

1. Lake Elementia (Kenya)
2. Lake Rudolf (Kenya)
3. Lake Nakuru (Kenya)
4. Lake Johann (Chad)
5. Lake Aranguadi (Ethiopia)
6. Lake Chiltu (Ethiopia)
7. Lake Buccacina (Peru)
8. Lake Texcoco (Mexico)

Now for the second set of the tests. This consisted of a series of tests designed to analyze the constituents of the strains through toxicity tests, culture tests, and the like. This scientific filter, as it were, was applied only to those strains which had succeeded in passing the first test. This was a most exhaustive and exhausting procedure, but both a perfectionism and a sense of the necessity of stringent tests in all aspects were strongly felt by us all since the development goal was so important. We were going to find the very best strain of Spirulina and apply to it the most advanced methods for pure-culturing it (culturing it without contamination), and to do this on a large-scale mass-production basis. Thus the tests had to be stringent.

At times, when failure followed upon failure, we felt an urge to throw our flasks against the wall in our frustration. But when we felt that way, a look through the microscope at the alluring form of Spirulina's movement would be sufficient to calm us down again. There were times when the members of the team would come to divergent conclusions or even three or four different conclusions from the data yielded by the experiments. We would stay up all night discussing the matter in the attempt to reach some agreement. Scientists cannot compromise. We debated our positions as best we could until an experiment could be set up the following day to test the various hypotheses. In this way the process of sifting, experimenting and weeding out candidates continued until only one remained—the strain of Spirulina which grew naturally on Lake Aranguadi in Ethiopia. It was the champion which had survived against odds of thirty-five to one.

Six outstanding features of DIC Spirulina

Why is the Spirulina grown in Ethiopia at Lake Aranguadi the champion variety, and what features does it have which the others did not? How does the product grown from this strain exhibit these "championship qualities"? This is the question I shall address myself to in this section, and I will do so by considering each characteristic in succession.

1. Ethiopian Spirulina is both clean and safe as a pure food product

The most crucial requirement of anything which is to be ingested as a food is that it be pure, hygienic. This means more than that it should merely appear clean upon visual inspection. There have to be thorough and complete hygiene controls and supervision over every aspect of the process from the quality of the raw materials to the production and distribution of the product. Let us start with an examination of the sanitary cleanliness of the original material.

Usually if one inspects the surface of algae growing in the sea one finds there a large variety of living bacteria growing. The slime covering the surface of the algae is a perfect breeding ground for other microscopic organisms. But if one studies the environmental conditions of the habitat of Spirulina one finds that all Spirulina is different in some interesting and important respects from other algae. The salt content of the salt lakes in which Spirulina grows is between ten and twenty percent (sea water is only three percent salt) and thus shows a strong alkaline character, with the most suitable temperature being between 32° and 42° Centigrade. In our research we discovered that the density of hydrogen ions most conducive to Spirulina's growth was in the range of 8.5-11 pH. When the density reached a pH of 11.5, growth was severely curtailed and when it went above a pH of 12 the Spirulina changed from its original blue-green color to brown and died. These are not conditions which allow the growth of most ordinary bacteria. Spirulina lives in a world apart, so to speak. Since Spirulina's ideal environment is one in which the normal bacteria cannot live, its habitat will not become contaminated by other microorganisms but will allow the Spirulina to grow in a truly clean and pure state.

Well then, what about the water conditions in Lake Aranguadi in Ethiopia? According to survey reports it possesses the most favorable conditions for growing Spirulina of all the candidates. The data reveal that the salt content is fifteen percent, pH level between 9 and 11, water temperature 32° C., and a sodium hydrogen carbonate (sodium bicarbonate) concentration of 1.6 percent. In short it has the ideal conditions for the growth of Spirulina. Thus, even in the natural state there is not any worry about adulteration of Ethiopian Spirulina by other bacteria and it is, consequently, safe to eat in its natural state.

2. DIC Spirulina is a pure culture from a sterile strain

Certainly, since Ethiopian Spirulina grows in a unique environ-ment which will not permit the growth of other organisms, it is found uncontaminated in its natural state. But what if it should happen that even a minute quantity of bacteria should somehow or other come into contact with the Spirulina at some point in the processing? This would be a serious source of pollution. Thus it is crucial to extract only the absolutely pure portion of the Spirulina cells and synthetically culture only this. This process is called "pure culturing" and it is this process that DIC applies to Ethio-pian Spirulina.

The pure culturing process is one which has many attendant difficulties and there were many failures to implement this process. But in the end we were once again saved to a large extent by the native properties of the Lake Aranguadi Spirulina itself. Specif-ically, since this variety of Spirulina is basically a tropical variety it has a strong tolerance for heat (thermophilic) and an ability to withstand ultraviolet radiation. These characteristics enabled our group, after many leads were followed, to finally resort to a process which combined heat control, exposure to ultraviolet radiation, and treatment with a medical fluid. This process allowed us to achieve a pure culture.

The pure culture operation is such that once even a particle of the microorganism, Spirulina, is successfully obtained in an unadulterated state it only remains to use that tiny bit as a basis for propagation.

3. Ethiopian Spirulina is large in size

In order to move to the next step of the process, the production of large quantities of the pure-cultured Spirulina, it is desirable to have the original Spirulina be of a large size, large at least for a microorganism. Fortunately, the Ethiopian Spirulina is 0.3 to 0.5 millimeters in length, which is large for a microorganism. Indeed, it is some 100 times larger than Chlorella, which is also an algae—so large that it can be seen with the naked eye.

The merit of being large is that this means that its propagational potential is high and that it is technically easy to harvest. It is obvious that when propagational potential is large it will be easier to achieve high production, but there is another factor to be considered. In the overall production process there is the operation of harvesting the propagated Spirulina from the culture pond. When the microorganism is of a small size, such as Chlorella, it is necessary to use a centrifuge to separate the subject organism from other material. This centrifuge procedure is simply not adequate to the demands of mass production because of the small amounts which can be handled at any one time. Mass production using this method would require large-scale apparatus and would mean the expenditure of large amounts of capital. In contrast, when we are dealing with a large form such as Spirulina, the separation can be accomplished by such primitive harvesting operations as scooping the algae from the surface of the water with a basket. This simplicity naturally has an effect on costs and is one of the most notable features of Ethiopian Spirulina.

An early picture of Professor Nakamura's own culture tanks on the roof of a house in 1963. The water is an intense green color.

Although this type of pond was used to grow Chlorella the same system can be used to grow Spirulina. Only the harvesting method is much simpler for Spirulina because it can be scraped off the sides or scooped out with nets or pumped through a mesh screen. Industrial methods of removal and separation have been developed.

The large drying and separation facilities of the Siam Algae Co. Ltd. These latest and most technically advanced ponds were designed by DIC to operate in an unpolluted environment.

4. Thailand: The world's best environment for Spirulina

No matter how great its propagational potential in itself, when one intends to artificially propagate the pure culture Spirulina for mass production it is necessary to have an environment and facilities which provide an appropriate industrial location for the propagation of the algae. It is relatively easy to state the requisite conditions—warm climate, clean air, and abundant water supply. Thailand, which DIC selected as the site for their breeding ground and factory, seems to have been created with the propagation of Spirulina in mind.

Thailand is blessed with the strong, bright sunlight of the tropics and even a child in elementary school knows that the sun's energy is indispensable for photosynthesis and the growing of plants. Spirulina is a photosynthetic plant whose growth and development is absolutely dependent on the supply of sunlight.

Moreover, the rainy season in Thailand is short, the proportion of sunlight hours in a day is quite high throughout the year, and the average temperature is also high.

Let us now consider the water supply, since large amounts of water are indispensable to cultivating Spirulina. The capital of Thailand, Bangkok, is so blessed with natural water that it is referred to as the "water capital." In order to get a clean water supply for their plant the DIC people went underground, 200 meters below the surface, to tap the pure underground water which is then pumped to the surface and sluiced to the culturing pond. Underground water is truly abundant in many places but there is perhaps no place in the world other than Thailand where it is so readily accessible for daily consumption. In any case, unlike river water, underground water is pure and unpolluted. It is not without reason that Japan's DIC is not alone in having set up food processing facilities in Thailand. For example, the German food processing company which makes Scenedesmus, also an algae product, selected Thailand as its culturing site. It is an ideal place for culturing algae. DIC's Thai plant is presently producing 100 tons of pure Spirulina each year.

5. The constituents of Spirulina are particles of protein with well-distributed amino acids

If the reader will look at the chart (1A) he will see that the constituent elements of Spirulina have truly superb nutritional value. Its most conspicuous characteristic is that protein constitutes about 70% of the total material. This is an astounding percentage and corresponds to 3½ times that of the protein content of beef or eggs. It is a superior food which is very clearly a pure mass of protein. But its superiority as a food is not due solely to the high percentage of protein for it would be useless to have all that protein if the amino acids which made it up were irregular, abnormal, or out of proportion. In this important respect there is no cause for worry since the array of amino acids in Spirulina is indeed well-balanced. One often hears the expression, "God certainly constructed this beautifully," when someone carefully considers human physiology or the function of the organs, and this expression would not be out of place for describing Spirulina.

When one looks at the constituent analysis of Spirulina one cannot but marvel at the intricate, ingenious distribution of the nutritional elements necessary to the maintenance of human life. This, too, is certainly one of God's masterpieces.

In addition, Spirulina contains large amounts of chlorophyll, and phycocyanin. As everyone knows chlorophyll is that which makes plants green and is referred to as "green blood". The carotenoids are called pro-vitamins or materials which change into Vitamin A. Phycocyanin is a type of bilirubin colorant which is peculiar to Spirulina, i.e., Spirulina has it but Chlorella does not. In any case having an abundance of these coloring agents is a characteristic peculiar to Spirulina, and it is for this reason that Spirulina exhibits its blue-green color.

Chart 1A
A) ANALYSIS OF SPIRULINA—ORGANIC CONSTITUENTS

Organic Constituent	Spirulina	Chlorella	Soy Bean
Protein	69.5%-71%	40-56%	39%
Carbohydrates	12.5%	10-25%	36%
Fats	8.0%	10-30%	19%
Vitamins	Provitamins, A, B_1, B_2, B_6, B_{12}, E Pantothenic Acid, Nicotinic Acid, Folic Acid	Provitamins, A, B_1, B_2, B_6, Nicotinic Acid	B_1, B_2, B_6
Coloring Agents	Chlorophyll Carotenoids Phycocyanin	Chlorophyll Carotenoids	

Chart 1B
B) SPIRULINA (DRY)—PROTEIN CONTENT COMPARED

Beef	18-20%	Soybean	33-35%
Eggs	10-25%	Fish (mackerel)	20%
Wheat	6-10%	Chlorella	40-56%
Rice	7%	Spirulina	69.5-71%

Chart 1C
C) SPIRULINA—RICH IN NECESSARY AMINO ACIDS

(amount per hundred grams)

Amino Acid	Spirulina	Chlorella	Soybean	Beef	Eggs	Mackerel	Standard
Isoleucine	3.3-3.9	3.9	1.8	0.93	0.67	0.83	4.2
Leucine	5.9-6.5	6.01	2.70	1.7	1.08	1.28	4.8
Lysine	2.6-3.3	3.6	2.58	1.76	0.89	1.95	4.2
Methionine	1.3-2.0	0.61	0.48	0.43	0.40	0.58	2.2
Cystine	0.5-0.7	0.48	0.48	0.23	0.35	0.38	4.2
Phenylalanine	2.6-3.3	3.00	1.98	0.86	0.65	0.61	2.8
Tyrosine	2.6-313	2.53	1.38	0.68	0.49	0.61	—
Threonine	3.0-316	2.30	1.62	0.86	0.59	0.99	2.8
Tryptophan	1.0-1.6	0.59	0.55	0.25	0.20	0.30	1.4
Valine	4.0-4.6	3.30	1.86	1.05	0.83	1.02	4.2

Chart 1D
D) SPIRULINA—MORE COLORING AGENTS AND MORE ABSORBENT THAN CHLORELLA

Colorant	Spirulina	Chlorella
Chlorophyll	1.6%	1.4%
Carotenoids	0.3%	0.2%
Phycocyanin	18.0%	0%

Chlorella is a simple cell covered with a thick cellular membrane. Spirulina is multicelled with a thin, weak membrane and thus it has good digestive absorption characteristics.

Synthetic Digestion Rate (2% pepsin for 48 hours)

	Spirulina	Chlorella
Digestive rate	95.1%	73.6%

6. Spirulina's mysterious power

For a scientist to talk about "mysterious power" is for him to court derision and ridicule, but this is in fact how I feel about Spirulina.

It is clear that the abundant nutrients (vitamins, minerals, etc.) found in Spirulina are in a well-balanced distribution indeed, but it is hard to believe that this alone can account for the dramatic therapeutic effects it has had. (See the other reports contained in this volume for details.)

Thinking upon this matter for some time I found myself speculating in the following manner. (This is speculation, not conclusions based on careful experiment.)

The blue-green algae, of which Spirulina is one, are very primitive plant forms. Some taxonomists distinguish them from other algae and place them in the class of nuclear plants (genkaku shikubutsu). Nuclear plants are those which are on the borderline between plants and animals, somewhat above the plants. The lactobacillus is regarded to be in this category. Indeed, Spirulina does not have the cellular wall characteristic of plants (thus its high digestibility!) and the nucleus is not well distinguished. In other words it is very close in structure to the first living things which appeared on the earth some billions of years ago. It was from those primitive life forms that all the plants and animal life on the earth today are descended. They were the fountain springs of life. Of course, Spirulina is not exactly like those life forms, but it is very close.

When one looks at Spirulina's helix, or spiral, form one gets the feeling that Spirulina too possesses the "vital power" of these primitive organisms and that this power has a beneficial effect on human beings also.

What I mean is that the spiral form is common to things as large as the galaxies in the heavens and as small as the microscopic form of the chromosomes in the cells, even down to RNA which transmits genetic information in the chromosomes. Thus this form could be called the "symbol of the mystery of nature."

If you ever have the chance to look at Spirulina through a microscope I think you too will come to feel that this speculation is not entirely unfounded.

The hope for increased therapeutic benefits more than the staple food of the future— use as the health food of the present

Let us turn to a discussion of the use and efficacy of Spirulina. Recently Spirulina has received much attention in newspapers, magazines and on television but the focus has always been on its potential as a food for the future. It is probably true that as the world population grows and food resources diminish we will be approaching an age characterized by a drastic food crisis, but here I want to consider Spirulina from a different perspective. It may be a future 'rice substitute' for people of the present day who are intimidated and oppressed by the unhealthy age in which they live.

Spirulina has been used in the clinical treatment of illness. In the present volume there are reports on these treatments by clinical specialists and I refer the reader to those studies for details. Here I will content myself with recording the facts that demonstrate remarkable results in the amelioration of a tremendous range of diseases from liver ailments and pancreatitis through anemia. This use in the medical treatment of disease is quite fine but I should also like to encourage its use by healthy people as a preventative measure against the so-called "adult diseases" and by those people who are on the verge of being diagnosed as having a full-fledged disease i.e., people with the following symptoms or conditions:

1. tire easily and worry about their health
2. catch cold easily
3. intake of green and yellow vegetables is not adequate
4. have dizzy spells
5. strong likes and dislikes which give rise to unbalanced nutrition
6. suffer broken bones under only minimal stress
7. don't eat breakfast

8. are dieting to reduce excessive weight
9. pregnant women

Spirulina—supplying alkaline balance to acid constitutions

The balanced nutritional composition of Spirulina will, of course, be effective in these instances, but over and above that it functions to modify the whole physical constitution. If one looks at the studies of people with illness-prone constitutions one finds that ninety percent have an acidic constitution. One hears the terms "alkaline" and "acid" constitution quite a bit these days but few people know precisely what these phrases signify. Let us turn to a simple explanation of these terms and their significance for us.

We take the elements of nutrition from food we eat to maintain our bodies and our lives, but in order for the food to become energy that we can use these elements must be burned in the body. However, this combustion produces by-products such as carbon dioxide and hydrogen ions. The carbon dioxide is directly expelled from our lungs as we exhale but the hydrogen ions combine with oxygen, flow into the blood and eventually are expelled in urine. When these hydrogen ions, which one might term the grime in the blood, remain in the blood in large numbers, one has what is called an acid constitution.

Since larger amounts of oxygen are required to evacuate the hydrogen ions in the blood from the body when their number increases, the result of this increase in population is to rob the body itself of oxygen to supply this need, and the effect of this is to leave the body oxygen-deficient. When the blood plasma is acidic one gets tired with even little exertion and one loses pep and vitality and eventually becomes listless. When this condition worsens one progresses to a full-fledged illness. This is the reason that an acid constitution is said to be the breeding ground of disease.

What then is the central cause of a person's having an acid constitution? Diet and stress are said to be the primary causes. When the diet is deficient in minerals such as sodium, potassium and magnesium a tendency towards acidity develops. Thus for the constitution to maintain alkalinity one must take in large amounts of these minerals. Of course, fundamentally, it is most desirable to obtain these minerals from one's daily food but since the end of World War II there has been a general westernization of the Japanese diet as well as a proliferation of processed foods, and thus one cannot hope to obtain sufficient amounts of these minerals from the ordinary diet. Spirulina, however, is rich in these minerals and thus is an ideal food for moderating and even changing this trend towards an acidic constitution.

Recent studies of children of elementary and middle school age show that there has been an unfortunate increase in the number of incidents of children becoming dizzy and fainting when morning exercises were just a bit longer than usual as well as an increase in the number of children who broke their legs from what seemed to be only a relatively gentle fall after only stumbling. Dizziness is the result of anemia, but what is of concern is not so much the number of children who have been formally diagnosed as being anemic as the alarming increase in the number of "borderline" cases where the students are just one step away from being anemic in the full sense. Furthermore, if one surveys these students one finds that almost all skip breakfast. I should really like to see these students try Spirulina.

Control health through food, not medicine

During the past ten years the Japanese have become quite insurance-conscious, and we are coming to the point where insurance is everybody's primary concern. But this does not seem to be true for questions of health, and there is just as much of a tendency to rely on medicine as there ever was.

Fundamentally, the Japanese character seems to be such that they simply like medicines. If we really desire to be healthy we must probably change this aspect of the "national character."

In any case as soon as a Japanese begins to feel a bit run down he immediately begins to clamor for a doctor, medicine, or an injection. Moreover there is a tendency not to believe that something is medicinal unless it is prescribed by a doctor.

This attitude, however, is undergoing something of a revision with the string of pharmaceutical disasters (e.g., Thalidomide) that have occurred recently. People are becoming increasingly critical of medication and drugs. This is evidence that the myth about the sanctity of medicine is being eroded.

This brings to mind Linus Pauling's Molecular Corrective Medicine. The phrase "Molecular Corrective Medicine" means that health is maintained and illness caused by a change in the concentration of substances which are normally present in the body and which are necessary to life. (From *Vitamin C, Colds, and Influenza.*)

In other words, medicines are foreign substances, basically poisons. Thus the treatment of illness should be based on changing the internal concentration of the life substances in the body rather than introducing foreign substances into the body. According to Pauling's thesis it is not desirable to use synthetic medicines because of the danger of side effects they might have. Rather it is most desirable to use substances which are naturally in the body and which are themselves necessary to life. This comes to the claim that health should be maintained and promoted, not through medication, but through proper diet.

If one concurs with this theory then one might say that Spirulina can become the fountainhead of health. It is a natural food with a balance of protein, minerals, vitamins, etc.; it has been certified safe and nontoxic; and there are no side effects even after repeated use. Moreover, since it is much more digestible than Chlorella, it is a perfect food for convalescence and recovering, maintaining and promoting health.

It gives me a good feeling to think of many Japanese receiving the joy of good health because of Spirulina, and it may be that the realization of this dream is not too far off in the future.

Use of microorganisms in World War I by the Germans

When one speaks of microalgae people usually think of Chlorella, but hereafter it will be the age of Spirulina, not Chlorella.

The attempt to mass-culture micro-organisms for use as food began during the first world war. It was a group of German scientists who tried to bring this idea into actuality at the request of the German Kaiser Wilhelm II.

At the time the Germans faced a drastic food shortage as the war intensified. Not only were the supplies of staple starches, grains, potatoes and the like drastically cut but they also were lacking in the meat, eggs and milk which supplied the normal protein for the diet. It came to the point where even animal feed had to be diverted for human use. All in all it was a very grave situation. The Kaiser thus ordered his scientists to find a new food source.

In response to this imperial request the scientists proposed to use edible yeasts and green algae, Chlorella, as the new food source. This edible yeast was developed by Professor M. Delbruch. He chose to produce a wild yeast, pale red in color and consequently known as "rose yeast". Later it was given the scientific name of rhodotorula.

The German government planned the industrial mass production of the rose-colored yeast to augment the extreme shortage of meat and dairy products, for, when compressed, the rose yeast resembled pork in appearance and color. Moreover, since it was superior to both pork and beef in its protein content it came to be known as "man-made meat". One wag even referred to the yeast as "a new breed of pig."

The development of this rose-colored yeast was the first step to making microorganisms into food. In fact some of the product was actually produced as a new food source, but before full mass production could begin Germany suffered defeat in the war.

Rose yeast was developed in 1917 and the next year Professor Lindner started work on turning the green algae, Chlorella, into food. Chlorella is an algae classified as a green algae. Because it synthesizes organic material with the aid of sunlight from water and air (carbon dioxide) it was also referred to as "air food."

If one compares Chlorella with an edible yeast such as rose yeast they display the following strengths and weaknesses:

The yeasts propagate well and thus are suitable for mass production, whereas Chlorella is deficient in this respect. The protein value of the yeast is also superior to that of Chlorella.

However, the culturing of yeast requires organic materials such as sugar while Chlorella needs only air, water, sunlight plus a small amount of minerals. Thus Chlorella was superior on this count. Further, Chlorella was better than the yeasts in terms of nutritional elements other than the protein.

Revival of interest in Chlorella with the Soviet and American space programs

Germany started the research on methods of mass-culturing Chlorella, but because this research started just at the time they lost the war the project was aborted. Nonetheless the German Chlorella research did succeed in stimulating the world's scientific community to take an interest in Chlorella.

Just after the first world war, in 1919, a German biochemist, Otto Walburg, conducted research on photosynthesis using Chlorella as a medium. He succeeded in doing some remarkable work. In Japan Dr. Mannen Shibata of Tohoku University accomplished for the first time a pure culturing of *Chlorella Elipoidera*. Prof. Shibata separated this Chlorella from the soil of the suburbs of Sendai and later the pure culture served as the foundation for subsequent Japanese research in Chlorella.

Eventually the second world war broke out in 1939 and the Germans at once started work on making food from the mass culturing of Chlorella, with Gottingen University's Prof. Herder given the responsibility for the research. However, the production of Chlorella ended in the test plan stage and never went into full mass production because the research center was totally demolished in a bombing raid. The only microorganism food to be mass produced in the second world war was an edible yeast, *torpsis utilis,* and further attempts to do something with Chlorella ended in failure.

Of course, both the Americans and the British, following the German lead, also made efforts to develop microorganisms as foodstuff during the second world war, but they also had more of an interest in the production of fats and oils from the microorganisms which dispersed the research.

Germany began the production of fats and oils from the mass culturing of diatom (silicious marl: Diatoom aceae) and they had some results with oil production from bacilli such as the thready yeast, *endomysesis, berunalysis,* and *fusalium.* Although the second world war ended in 1945 there still was a concern over the possibility of a worldwide food shortage because of an insufficient supply of protein sources brought about by the population expansion and the agricultural devastation of the war.

Thus the Carnegie Foundation in the U.S. conducted research led by Professor Spore into the making of food from Chlorella. Professor Spore felt that countries like Japan should be encouraged to look into the mass production of Chlorella in order to really make a breakthrough in the world food crisis.

In 1951, experimental research on the mass culturing of Chlorella started in Japan at the Tokugawa Research Institute (dissolved in 1970). In 1957 the Japanese government, at America's urging, developed a plan to independently mass produce Chlorella and set aside funds for scientific and technical research. The Japan Chlorella Research Institute was established in the same year at Kunitachi. This research institute is part of the Japan Dietary Association (Nihon Shokuseikatsu Kyokai, Kiichi Minami, Managing Director) but the director of the center was made directly responsible to the managing director himself, and I, as one of the board, was appointed assistant director in 1957.

The JCR Institute adopted the open-stirring method developed by the Tokugawa Research Institute and constructed an outdoor culture pond of 4000 square meters to begin the culturing process in 1958. The goal was set at a yearly production of twelve tons (dry weight), and it was, at that time, the largest operation of its kind in the world.

Subsequently, with the general amelioration of the food situation it almost seemed that Chlorella had been forgotten, but suddenly the Russians launched the first successful manned satellite and Chlorella again gained considerable attention, this time as a possible food source for space travel. Both America and the Soviet Union pursued intensive research into efficient methods of culturing Chlorella so that it could serve as a self-sufficient food supply in space vessels on long journeys.

The Japan Chlorella Institute was a nonprofit research organization, but when the supplementary funds supplied by the government were discontinued, administration of the Institute became exceedingly difficult. Ultimately it was disbanded in 1963 with the land and all facilities being transferred to the parent Yakult Corporation.

However, since the constituent elements of Chlorella were always therapeutically effective, interest in Chlorella as a health food began at about this time. In 1964 Chlorella Industries and several other companies were established, all with the purpose of producing Chlorella as a "natural food"! Today more than 100 companies are involved with Chlorella as a product in some fashion or other.

Spirulina—better than Chlorella on three counts:
a) harvesting   b) nutrition   c) digestibility

We have focused thus far on Chlorella as a profitable enterprise but did not mention a number of bottlenecks which then restricted the production of Chlorella in large quantities.

The first difficulty is that Chlorella is a tiny monocellular algae whose size is only 5 microns. This means that the harvesting requires a centrifuge operation which entails enormous expenditure of both time, labor and electric power. Because Chlorella is so minute one has to use a high-speed centrifuge, and such an apparatus uses large quantities of electricity. The second problem is that Chlorella is not easily digested because of its thick cellular membrane. There have been numerous research projects concerned to upgrade the digestive rate of Chlorella but as yet the problem has not been really solved.

It was at this juncture that Spirulina came on the scene. Spirulina was introduced into Japan in 1970 and had been nothing more than just another unknown algae prior to that. But in fact, Spirulina is superior to Chlorella in a number of important respects.

First, Spirulina is multicellular with a size 100 times that of Chlorella and thus there is no necessity to have a centrifuge operation as part of the harvesting procedure. Indeed one can simply harvest it with a filter cloth. Thus the various bottlenecks which clogged the path of mass production of tiny algae are just not there in the case of Spirulina. It can be farmed by anyone with a scoop.

Secondly, Spirulina's membrane is thin, making it very easy to digest. Digestibility was a vexing problem with Chlorella, but not with Spirulina. In tests of Spirulina's digestibility made with the proteinase pepsin, about 85% is digested in 16 hours. In short, Spirulina has about twice the digestibility of Chlorella.

Moreover, Chlorella is cultivated in weakly acidic conditions whereas Spirulina, on the contrary, grows well in very alkaline conditions. The effect of this difference is particularly noticeable in the carbon dioxide supply.

When a culture solution is acidic, the major portion of the aspirated (generated) carbon dioxide escapes into the atmosphere and only a very small amount is dissolved and utilized. But in the case of an alkaline culture solution the carbon dioxide gas is transformed into hydrogen carbonate ions which remain in the solution. Thus the percentage which escapes into the atmosphere is low. Spirulina thus can absorb not only carbon dioxide but also hydrogen carbonate ions as a source of carbon.

Having a high efficiency in the utilization of carbon dioxide is a big plus for Spirulina and it means that its practicality is much higher than that of Chlorella.

I would judge that future microalgae enterprises will gradually concentrate on Spirulina rather than Chlorella.

PART II

SPIRULINA'S ASTOUNDING THERAPEUTIC EFFICACY

Astonishing clinical examples of success with diabetes, liver disease and gastroenteric disorders, as reported in medical practice by several prominent Japanese doctors.

Chapter Three

REMARKABLE EFFECTS ON THE PROBLEM DISEASES OF OUR TIME— DIABETES, HEPATITIS, ANEMIA, ETC.

Spirulina perfect for improving the bodies and dispositions of the Japanese people.

by Dr. Tadaya Takeuchi, Ph.D., M.D.
National Medical and Dental University of Tokyo

Experiments with the problem diseases that up-to-date medicine can't cure

I should like to write as simply and concisely as possible about the clinical effects of Spirulina use on diseases of the liver, diabetes, and anemia.

I began using Spirulina in clinical contexts when requested to do so experimentally by Prof. Kazuo Takemoto of the Saitama Medical College.

Professor Takemoto had been in charge of the toxicity tests made on the Spirulina pure-cultured in Thailand by the Greater Japan Ink and Chemical Co. Ltd. These tests had proved that Spirulina had no toxic character whatever.

Acting on his suggestion I actually administered Spirulina to patients and found that it did indeed have a beneficial effect on a variety of diseases from diabetes and anemia through liver disease and stomach ulcers. Thus I have come to the point of setting down on paper the results of that course of treatment, but before I do so I have been requested by the editors to explain the relation between Spirulina and disease in a way that will be clear and intelligible to the general public rather than simply write a narrow, technical article.* For this reason I have decided to start with a consideration of the general question, "Why is a food like Spirulina necessary for modern man?" and then go on to examine the clinical results of using Spirulina with patients suffering from various illnesses.

---

* The editor of the English edition received a series of confidential papers by Professor Takeuchi on Spirulina with reference to hyperchromic anemia, diabetes mellitus and acute toxicity studies in early 1979 from DIC but was prevented from publishing them at that time because of the forthcoming issue of this book. However, the toxicity studies on rats and mice, which are technically detailed and lengthy, have therefore not been included in this volume.

Remarkable effects on diseases like diabetes and hepatitis which medicine can't cure

Shigenobu Okuma once propounded the thesis that the natural human life span should be 125 years. Even if we are still a long way from that goal it nonetheless is true that the average lifespan of the Japanese since World War II has lengthened considerably.

The average life expectancy is the number of years an average baby born in a given year can expect to live. According to the material I have at hand, the Ministry of Health and Welfare first computed the average life expectancy of the Japanese in the Meiji period, and if one looks at the first chart (Meiji 24-31, i.e. 1891-98) the figures given are 42.8 for males and 44.3 for females.

This kind of "Young society" with an average life expectancy of less than 50 continued for some time and only after the second world war did the life expectancy rise above 50—for women in 1946 and for men in 1947.

Since the war, with the resurgence of the economy, better diet and advances in medical technology, the life expectancy of the Japanese has shown an astounding increase, so that in 1978 it reached 72.97 for males and 78.33 for females. Now, too, for the first time the number of citizens 65 years of age or older has passed the 10 million mark, which constitutes 8.9% of the population: We have finally become a "mature society!"

However, the enemies of long life are the "adult" diseases of stroke, cancer, and heart disease. Once these diseases are conquered it is estimated that the average life expectancy will be extended by 7.44 years for males and 7.39 for females.

It is obviously a good thing to have the life expectancy lengthened in this fashion, but it is not an unmixed blessing, for when this happens there is a dramatic increase in deaths resulting from cirrhosis of the liver and diabetes. If one looks at the "top ten" causes of death in Japan, cerebral apoplexy, cancer and heart disease hold the first three positions as one might expect, but since

1976 cirrhosis of the liver and diabetes have "made it into the big time," as it were, by becoming the 9th- and 10th-ranking fatal diseases. Pulmonary tuberculosis, on the other hand, which had formerly been regarded with great fear because it was incurable, disappeared from the list completely.

Why did TB drop from the list to be replaced by diabetes and cirrhosis? TB is caused by the tubercle bacillus, and with the development of antibiotics such as streptomycin and PAS (aminosaliaylic acid) which kill that bacillus, the disease is now fully under control.

Thus TB can almost be said to be a disease which "can be cured with an injection." This, of course, is a gross oversimplification and not all cases are so easily treatable, but the phrase does highlight the direction of treatment in the ideal case. In contrast, liver disease and diabetes are by no stretch of the imagination diseases which can be cured with an injection. The same is true of anemia. These are diseases which cannot be cured merely by taking medication prescribed by a doctor.

Since the various functions of the organs break down for a variety of reasons, there is no hope of restoring them to a fully operative state with a simple injection, and it is this fact which makes their treatment difficult. More explicitly stated, they are diseases such that the physician's medicine alone cannot restore normal functioning to the damaged organ.

Thus, when I heard of Spirulina from Professor Takemoto and considered its constituent elements I judged that Spirulina might have some beneficial effect if used by patients suffering from anemia and diabetes. This was in September 1977.

Subsequently, remarkable results were achieved when Spirulina was employed as a supplement to the normal treatment. From the beginning the decision to use Spirulina in a clinical setting was made only because of our knowledge of its purity and against the background of its safety as demonstrated by inspection of the total data from the toxicity tests conducted by Professor Takemoto for a period of six months.

Its therapeutic value was far greater than anyone anticipated. I had expected Spirulina to have some effect simply because of its composition, but the results of the clinical tests went far beyond anything I had expected or hoped for. At this point it would be best to close this perhaps too long introduction and ask the reader to refer to the next section for the details of our studies.

A report of recovery—in two months blood sugar levels of diabetics return to near-normal.
Diabetes is an inability to break down too much sugar in the bloodstream.

In order to maintain our health it is necessary to continually ingest nutritional elements, change them internally, make energy, and repair the body's constituent material. The nutritional elements include protein, sugar, fats, vitamins and minerals (inorganic).

Normal, healthy people can get along quite well even if they don't eat for twenty-four hours or so. Because of this they seldom have any interest in computing how much of which of these five nutritional elements they are taking in at a meal or in a day. Nonetheless they maintain their health. They do so because there is a mechanism in the body which, according to its need, demands certain elements, stores them when they are present in excessive amounts, and uses this excess to make up for deficiencies when they occur. This mechanism is none other than the liver.

However when there is a great deficiency in the intake of nutrients over a prolonged period this mechanism gradually starts to malfunction and this will eventually manifest itself as a full-fledged illness. One of these diseases is diabetes.

Diabetes is a metabolic disorder which occurs because of an insufficient activity of the hormone insulin. If the amount of insulin is low its total activity will of course be low, but even more importantly there can occur instances when, for some reason, the insulin does not perform its proper function even though it is present in what should be sufficient quantities.

Just as gasoline is necessary for the running of an automobile, so, too, in order for us to be active our bodies must have glucose (blood sugar) in the blood to act as a fuel.

The sugar contained in food must be changed into the form of glucose to enter the bloodstream and be carried to various parts of the body. For this sugar to supply energy that we need it must enter the muscle and fat tissue and be stored there to be burned up as energy. Insulin plays an important role in this process.

At any rate, diabetes is a state of insulin deficiency. When insulin is insufficient it becomes very difficult to break down the glucose and convert it to energy. When that happens our bodies break down fats or protein instead of sugar to fill the demand for energy. Thus, diabetes is not just a metabolic disorder with reference to the sugar alone, but rather is a metabolic disorder which encompasses the role of the fats and protein also. The representative symptoms of diabetes are "high level of blood sugar" and glucosuria (sugary urine).

On an empty stomach the glucose level in the blood is about 0.1% (100 milligrams per deciliter) but when the glucose level increases much beyond this the glucose is discharged into the urine. When, on the contrary, the blood sugar level drops, glycogen, which is stored in the liver, is broken down into glucose, released into the blood and then sent to all parts of the body to be stored in the muscle tissue until it eventually is burned off to make energy. The liver synthesizes excess glucose to polysaccharides like glycogen and stores it for just this purpose.

Thus glucose is supplied by the liver and consumed in the muscle tissue and when both supply and consumption are in balance the glucose in the blood maintains a normal value. In diabetics, however, this balance is destroyed, the rate at which the blood sugar enters the muscle tissue is lower and the blood sugar level rises. The cause of this is an inadequate functioning of insulin.

When insulin activity is insufficient there is first a rise in the glucose level in the blood which decreases the total combustion of glucose in the muscle cells and results in a lack of sufficient energy supply.

In order to rectify this state the neutral fats stored in the fat tissue and protein from the muscle tissue is broken down to help produce energy to make up what is missing. This is why diabetes cannot simply be regarded as a metabolic abnormality of the sugar. This then is the set of physical principles underlying the occurrence of diabetes and I hope that my explanation has been sufficiently clear to give the general reader an understanding of it.

Let us now turn to the subjectively experienced symptoms of diabetes, their causes and the therapeutic effects Spirulina has been seen to have when used in its treatment.

Food control—the basic treatment for diabetes is dietary treatment

There are some who claim that there are no subjective symptoms of diabetes, but in fact the patient usually tends to drink quite a bit more liquid than normal because his throat becomes easily parched. Moreover, the patient urinates frequently, waking up often in the middle of the night to go to the bathroom, and never seems to feel full no matter how much he eats. He tires quite easily, both puts on weight very quickly and loses it just as suddenly. His sexual appetite declines, his skin is easily roughened, and he tends to become nervous.

Now these subjective symptoms do not always appear together but if the reader finds that some of them are quite familiar to him it would be best for him to consult a physician. It is important to have one's urine checked only after more than two full hours have passed after a meal.

If diabetes is not attended to then a number of other illnesses break out as a consequence of the metabolic imbalances set up. Diabetic glaucoma is a very vexatious disease for which early detection and treatment is quite important. It is also true that diabetes in children has recently become much more frequent, so it behooves one to be careful to attend to the warning signs.

I have already said that the cause of diabetes is a deficiency of insulin and thus the appropriate strategy for treatment would be to find a method to rectify that deficiency. There are three methods designed to do this:

1. reduce the demand for insulin in the body
2. encourage the production of more insulin in the body
3. supply extra insulin from outside the body

Both the second and third methods rely on medicines of one sort or other, but the most effective, least complicated, and most reasonable method is the first, i.e., economically using the insulin already present.

Among the causes of increased demand for insulin are lack of exercise, stress and liver disorders, but the most prevalent causes by far are overeating and obesity. The more one eats and the more obese one becomes, the more necessary it is to have large quantities of insulin since it is the insulin which regulates the metabolism and breaks down sugar. In order to conserve insulin and not to waste it one should hold the daily caloric intake to the minimal acceptable level and make every effort to maintain one's ideal weight.

One method of calculating one's approximate ideal weight in kilograms is to subtract 100 from one's height in centimeters* and then multiply the result by 0.9. Thus for a person who was 154 cm. (5'½") in height the result would be 48.6 kg. (107 lbs.) Self-control through diet is a matter of supreme importance for health.

There is no doubt whatever that diet is absolutely the first

---

* One inch equals 2.54 centimeters; one kilogram equals 2.2 pounds.

priority in the treatment of diabetes, since it is not the sort of disease which can be cured by a mode of treatment which consists only of medication and injection. Whether the treatment is successful or not is almost completely dependent on whether the patient can continue a proper dietary therapy as he goes on through life.

Strictly speaking, there are two parts to a therapy centered on diet. There is the therapy diet itself and the maintenance diet. The therapy diet is a strictly regulated 1200 calorie diet which is designed to contain a balance of the various necessary nutrients in minimal amounts. The diet is adjusted under supervision as the treatment progresses and when the circumstances warrant, the calorie count may be raised, if to do so would be beneficial. Eventually the patient will be permitted to progress from the therapy diet to a maintenance diet where the caloric intake is usually set at about 1600 calories depending on the patient's basic metabolism and energy expenditure. In this dietary treatment the physician sets the total caloric intake, but it would be a grave mistake to think that this leaves the patient free to eat anything he wants within these limits, for throughout the entire program it is crucial that the patient be supplied with sufficient amounts of all the essential nutrients.

Dramatic improvement in diabetics thanks to Spirulina

In a series of clinical tests we prescribed Spirulina to be taken along with a strict, nondiscretionary diet to rather seriously afflicted diabetic patients, and achieved many significant results. We administered 7 tablets at a time, 3 times a day for a total of 21 tablets per day. The results speak for themselves as the following case histories will demonstrate. See Case Chart II.

Case I: Male, 48 years old, office worker, height 167 cm., weight 75 kg. No unusual medical history.

This patient's job environment was such that there were many occasions when he drank alcoholic beverages in connection with business. He tended to favor whiskey at these times and was the type who drank without nibbling on "party foods" or snacks. In a general physical examination it was determined that his blood sugar level with an empty stomach was 128, indicating a mild case.

The method of treatment consisted of weight control through a pattern of exercise and a Spirulina-supplemented diet. By the 60th day his blood sugar level returned to normal.

Case II: Male, 55 years old, Taxi driver, height 168 cm., weight 70 kg. Medical history: Patient had been hospitalized for 6 months at age of 21 for tuberculosis. Received internal treatment.

The patient did not drink alcohol at all in connection with his job but he did have quite a sweet tooth, irregular eating habits and difficult meal patterns. In addition, cataracts, which often seem to be associated with diabetes, developed in both eyes.

The treatment consisted of a thorough-going therapeutic diet with Spirulina supplement. The patient was exceedingly faithful in following the direction of the therapists and in 60 days the blood sugar level had returned to normal.

Case III: Male, 56 years old, office worker, height 164 cm., weight 56 kg., blood pressure 188/96. He was receiving a diuretic pressure depressant from a local clinic and had succeeded in lowering the higher figure to less than 150.

This patient had a rather high blood sugar level of 212 with an empty stomach and a figure of 380 on the two-hour-after test. Because of this high value there was some question as to whether medication should be used to lower the glucose level. The reason for the hesitancy was that the range of medication that one can use with a patient like this is extremely restricted. It seemed that nothing could be done. In cases like this where it seems that normal treatment will be ineffective there is a tendency to resort to medication. The difficulty with this approach is that once the patient starts on some form of medication it becomes difficult for him to stop.

CHART II

Case I: 50 g. Glucose Load Blood Sugar Test

	Before Initial Treatment	After 30 days	60 days	Normal Value
Empty Stomach	128	116	96	(Under 100)
30 min. after meal	158	162	154	
60 min. ,,	206	168	160	(Under 170)
90 min. ,,	172	130	122	
120 min. ,,	134	104	94	(Under 120)

Case II: Same Conditions as Above

Empty Stomach	176	122	102	(Under 100)
30 min. after meal	212	200	168	
60 min. ,,	238	236	170	(Under 170)
90 min. ,,	196	174	136	
120 min. ,,	136	120	98	(Under 120)

Case III: Same Conditions As Above

Empty Stomach	212	172	180	(Under 100)
30 min. after meal	266	194	206	
60 min. ,,	354	226	198	(Under 170)
90 min. ,,	360	202	180	
120 min. ,,	380	178	146	(Under 120)

(In all these cases the "meal" consisted of 50 grams of glucose given to patients on an empty stomach. Changes in the level of blood sugar were tested then at the intervals indicated.)

Thus we decided to hold off on the medication and see what results could be achieved with Spirulina and exercise. After 30 and 60 days positive results were observed with the sugar nearly disappearing from the urine and the subjective symptoms subsiding.

Diabetes cannot be cured but can be controlled

Among the statements made by the American Professor Joslyn is the famous, "Diabetes cannot be cured but it can be controlled." While on the one hand this seems to be a harsh pronouncement since it tells patients that their disease is incurable, yet on the other hand it does at least offer the consolation that the patient can live a nearly normal existence if he but exercise self-control. It is a source, thus, of encouragement for these patients.

I always repeat this statement to my diabetic patients. Anyone who is diabetic should know that the basic rule of diabetic treatment is the combination of exercise and diet in a therapy program. Nonetheless there are still patients who continue their unhealthy way of living because they can't understand this simple fact or because they cannot put the principles into practice even though they understand them.

In connection with this it is clear that if a patient takes Spirulina as prescribed he can be assured of acquiring the necessary elements of nutrition in sufficient amounts. It is extremely simple. Since it is an alkaline food it can be the basis for harmoniously metabolizing the nutritional elements in the body.

In any event, diabetes is a disease which requires patience and perseverance in the course of the treatment. Fundamentally it is a disease which can be successfully treated only with the full cooperation of the doctor, the patient, and the patient's family.

In the cases which were part of our study, the combination of the patients following our direction, exercising strict self-control and taking Spirulina as prescribed, led to great improvement in the blood sugar level.

Better results than prescription medicine in cases of anemia.
Death is a possibility with anemia also.

People suffering from anemia tend to display a variety of symptoms varying with each individual and ranging from loss of color in the face, heavy-headedness, dizziness, ringing in the ears, becoming tired easily and loss of stamina. Especially when climbing stairs, in the subway for instance, they experience heart palpitations and shortness of breath. When the anemia worsens there is sometimes a swelling of the feet and hands.

Blood is composed of red corpuscles, white corpuscles, blood platelets and organic elements, as well as blood plasma. One can think of the red and white corpuscles mixed together with the blood platelets in the plasma.

In cases of anemia the red corpuscle count (normally 450-500 per cc. for males and 400-450 per cc. for females) decreases, or if there is no decrease in the actual number of red corpuscles there is a decrease in the amount of hemoglobin they contain.

The primary function of the red corpuscles is to transport oxygen, and what allows them to perform this function is the activity of the hemoglobin. When the blood circulates through the lungs it takes oxygen from the pulmonary alveoli (the air cells in the lungs) which combines with the hemoglobin in the blood cells. The blood then, while flowing through the capillaries throughout the body, supplies this oxygen to the tissue. The blood also then absorbs the carbon dioxide generated by the tissues' breathing, returns this to the lungs and releases it in the pulmonary alveoli.

In anemia, since the red corpuscle count and the amount of hemoglobin* decline, the efficiency of the oxygen-carbon dioxide transfer exchange operation between the lungs and tissue is lowered. This means the tissues cannot breathe properly.

---

* Normal is 15 g. per deciliter, but when there is less than 13 g. for males or 12 g. for females, anemia results from iron deficiency.

The red corpuscles are manufactured in the bone marrow out of protein and iron. At this time they take in vitamins B1, B6, B12, C and others as nutrients. These red corpuscles then enter the bloodstream and travel throughout the entire body (a trip of approximately 280 km.) to be finally broken down and disposed of in the liver and spleen after 120 days or so. After they are broken down the iron is again conveyed to the bone marrow to serve as material for new red corpuscles while the other elements are further broken down into bilirubin (bile pigment) to be expelled from the body as waste. If this process is obstructed at any point along the way, anemia results.

As we have seen, if the amount of hemoglobin diminishes, an oxygen shortage occurs, and this results in an anemic condition with the symptoms discussed earlier making their appearance. That is to say, the patient becomes easily tired. If this state of affairs continues for a prolonged period there is the danger of death being the ultimate result. Thus anemia is not a disease to be lightly dismissed.

What then is the cause of this sometimes fatal disease, anemia? Three basic causes can be stated.

Anemia results from dietary irregularity and food disorders

The three major causes of anemia are:

1. Blood loss
2. Iron deficiency. Hemoglobin is the result of a material which is a combination of an iron (heme) and porphyrin uniting with globulin. Anemia occurs when there is a shortage of iron because of the fact that iron is an essential constituent of hemoglobin.
3. Decline in the blood-producing function

Now there are basically two types of anemia: a) iron-deficiency anemia and, b) acute (malignant) anemia, and we shall examine each in turn.

a. Iron-deficiency Anemia

Iron-deficiency anemia is the most prevalent sort, covering 85% of all cases. Most of the one in four women who are said to be anemic have iron deficiencies. This is particularly a problem for young women, such as co-eds and office workers in the 18-25 year old range, who have a 25-40% rate of anemia, as compared with the general female population which is one in four.

The reason for this high incidence of anemia among young women is explained quite simply in terms of poor diet. For a bewildering variety of reasons some people fall into poor dietary habits. They skip breakfast to lose weight or keep their figure, indulge too much in the drinking of cold drinks and the eating of convenience foods. They develop habits which are heavily oriented towards sugars, and it is in just this sort of person that anemic symptoms are so common.

Over and above these factors there is the fact that women tend to lose more iron than men because of menstruation and giving birth. Since the woman's body needs extra amounts of iron to develop the body of the fetus within during a pregnancy, it is not surprising that anemia would be more generally common among females than males.

Other forms of blood loss also give rise to anemia, e.g., blood loss from external injuries, surgery, stomach or duodenal ulcers, or hemorrhoids may be causes.

The diet prescribed for an anemic condition requires the intake of high calorie, high vitamin and high protein foods as well as a sufficient supply of iron and other blood-building material. In other words, such a diet calls for meat, vegetables, and fruits in abundance supplemented by eggs and milk. Coffee and tea are prohibited foods while one is on such an iron-rich diet. This is because the alkaloids they contain combine with the iron and make it harder to absorb.

b. Malignant or Acute Anemia

In times past there have been instances where an anemic

patient gradually weakened and died because the cure for anemia was not known and no form of treatment seemed to be effective.

Since, however, the raw liver treatment was developed by Minot in 1926 this is not the case any longer and the disease itself seems to have a relatively low incidence rate in Japan.

The cause of this disease is a deficiency of vitamin B12 and for this reason a high protein, high vitamin diet is effective in treating it. If, however, a B12 dosage treatment is employed (this is the essence of Minot's liver treatment), then there is no necessity to develop such a diet.

When the anemia is due to malnutrition, one sometimes finds enlarged hemocyte anemia, and since this particular form of anemia is caused by a lack of vitamin B12 or folic acid, supplying these is extremely effective in this type of case.

In any case, there are many women who skip breakfast and have nothing but a sandwich and coffee for lunch simply because they want to regain or maintain their figure, with the result that they do not get the necessary vitamins, protein or iron. If such an inadequate diet is continued they will eventually become anemic. In such cases, I thought, Spirulina could help restore the balance of nutritional elements in the diet since it is so rich in the iron needed to make blood, and also has good quality protein which contains the required amino acids, and minerals as well.

Nine cases where Spirulina was more effective than previous medication

As subjects for the treatment we selected 9 people (1 male and 8 female) from the general out-patient population. All the subjects had "low coloration" (paleface) anemia without complications. The administered dosage was 20 tablets after each meal.

The subjects did not have any particular abnormality in their red blood cell count, their hemoglobin level was under 12 gm. per deciliter, and the hematocrit under 39%. Hematocrit is a ratio of packed red blood cells to the volume of whole blood expressed in percent. Their ages ranged from 18 to 47. See Chart III.

Most of the subjects were young women and when they were examined it was found that they followed, for cosmetic reasons, those unreasonably low calorie diets which tended to be low in protein and high in sugar. Of the subjects only the 47 year old male had had blood loss problems, due to hemorrhoids, and thus could not be said to have been simply a case of "low coloration" anemia.

From our experience with these cases it can be definitely stated that Spirulina was far superior to previous medication therapy in treating an anemia of this sort which results from insufficient intake of trace nutritional elements. Such an inadequate diet is quite common these days, so the conclusion is obvious.

The reason Spirulina is so successful is that, unlike iron medication, it is a natural food which contains high quality protein as well as various vitamins and minerals, and consequently, there are no abnormal effects even after prolonged use.

As you can see from Chart III the effects of the Spirulina diet in all cases were apparent after 15-30 days. This provides good evidence for the view that Spirulina is an ideal supplementary food for one suffering from anemia arising from nutritional deficiencies.

The preventative administration of Spirulina— great efficacy in the prevention and treatment of chronic and acute hepatitis, viral hepatitis

Hepatitis is a disease which is said to have a number of causes including infection, spoiled food, excessive drinking and poisoning.

Of the infections, those by virus are the most prevalent and the virus is generally referred to as the hepatitis virus, which comes in two forms, A and B.

CHART III

SPIRULINA'S EFFECT ON SYMPTOMS OF ANEMIA

(This chart gives the data for changes in the red cell count (r), hemoglobin (Hb) and hematocrit (Ht) from before treatment, 15 days, 30 days, 45 days after treatment began.)

			Before (in millions)	15 days	30 days	45 da
Case I	Female, 18 years	R	3.85	3.9	3.88	3.9
		Hb	10.6	11.6	13.0	13.1
		Ht	35	38	39	39
Case II	Female, 19	R	3.95	3.94	3.98	4.0
		Hb	11.0	11.9	12.4	12.1
		Ht	34	35	37	37
Case III	Female, 19	R	4.1	4.06	4.12	4.0
		Hb	10.6	12.6	13	13.2
		Ht	34	37	38	38
Case IV	Female, 20	R	4.06	3.98	4.00	4.0
		Hb	10.8	12.2	13.9	13.8
		Ht	35	37	39	39
Case V	Female, 22	R	3.9	3.98	4.00	3.9
		Hb	11.0	13.0	13.3	13.2
		Ht	37	38	39	39
Case VI	Female, 22	R	3.96	4.01	4.10	4.0
		Hb	11.2	12.6	13.9	14.0
		Ht	36	38	39	39
Case VII	Female, 25	R	3.96	4.02	4.10	4.0
		Hb	10.8	11.0	12.0	13.2
		Ht	35	37	37	38
Case VIII	Female, 31	R	4.08	4.10	4.00	4.0
		Hb	11.6	13.0	14.4	14.0
		Ht	37	37	39	40
Case IX	Male, 47	R	4.20	4.36	4.26	4.2
		Hb	13.0	14.6	15.8	15.6
		Ht	39	43	43.5	44

The normal values are: Red cells (R) ($10^6/m^3$) Male 4.4–5.6 million,
Female 3.8-5.2 million
Hemoglobin (Hb) (g/dl) Male 12-16
Hematocrit (Ht) (%) Male 40-48, Female 34-42

The form caused by virus A is called epidemic hepatitis with an incubation period of 10-40 days. Not all of the infected individuals actually come down with the disease but when the disease does manifest itself it usually does so in those who are physically or emotionally tired or those who have vitamin or protein deficiencies.

If a person under 40 starts suddenly to catch colds or develop gastrointestinal problems which eventually lead to jaundice, and if he or she has not been taking some sort of medication prior to the occurrence of those symptoms it is most likely that he or she is afflicted with type A hepatitis.

Type B hepatitis is also called blood serum (lymph) hepatitis and usually breaks out as a result of an infection gotten during a blood transfusion. The virus enters the body and incubates for at least over three weeks before the symptoms occur. Thus even six months after a transfusion there still remains the danger of an outbreak of the disease.

There is, moreover, a positive correlation between the increased consumption of strong alcoholic beverages (those with high alcohol content) and the rate of incidence of liver disease. When one inquires into the causal relationship between these two, one finds that there is as yet no evidence that the alcohol directly attacks the liver cells themselves, rather it is thought that the alcohol does its work by causing a nutritional disorder.

Now to consider the treatment of this disease. First of all it must be said that there is no medicine which is effective against viral hepatitis. The major burden of any treatment plan is placed on absolute rest and a nutritional approach, i.e., a high vitamin and high protein diet. In this case medicine is only an aid or assistant in the treatment. No matter how slight the symptoms may be, three weeks absolute rest is a must.

In the early stages, when the patient's appetite is low, the nutrients are supplied intravenously or by injection. The protein must be one which contains the essential animo acids, and there must be 1.5-2 grams taken in for each kilogram of body weight. If the high quality protein is supplemented by abundant vitamins repair of the liver cells is possible. In the past a high protein, high vitamin, high calorie diet was recommended in these cases but now it is generally recognized that the high caloric intake is not necessary. Thus the present standard is set at 300-400 grams of sugar and 30-60 grams of fats with this level being adjusted according to age and body weight.

Effects on both chronic and acute hepatitis

Spirulina was given to four subjects with type A hepatitis and two with type B for a total of six patients in the study. All were selected from the out-patients of the clinic. Two of the type A patients had acute hepatitis while the other two type A, as well as both the type B patients, were patients continuing to visit the clinic after release from the hospital.

The Spirulina dosage was seven tablets three times a day for a total of twenty-one daily. Apart from the nutritionist's direction of diet and the Spirulina, no medication whatever was used in the study.

A battery of tests was given every two weeks which included blood tests and liver function tests. These were broken down into eight categories: 1) Total protein (TP), 2) Total cholesterol (TC), 3) Jaundice index (MG), 4) Glutamic acid, oxyalacetic acid, transaminase (GOT), 5) Glutamic acid, pyruvic acid, transaminase (GPT), 6) Thymol reaction (TTT), 7) Kunckel reaction (ZTT), and 8) Alkali phosphatase (AIP).

The results clearly showed that in all cases of this Spirulina treatment, the liver functions were greatly improved, either being completely restored and cured or at least brought back into the normal range.

It is particularly notable that in all cases the serum protein level noticeably increased and the effect on the cholesterol level was such that the initially low levels were increased while those that had been too high were lowered. In all patients the cholesterol levels returned close to the ideal value of 180-220 mg. per cc. of blood.

In the acute hepatitis cases the GOT and GPT began to improve after only two weeks and by six weeks had returned to normal levels. Improvement was also noted in the four cases of chronic hepatitis.

These findings were the result of Spirulina's ability to provide high quality protein and vitamins to the patients. The reason for thinking this is that the serum cholesterol levels were found to improve as the serum protein level was elevated.

The liver, when performing its functions normally, is fresh and clean-looking, with a yellowish brown color. When, for some reason, its functions are impaired it first begins to swell in size. If at this point in time the affected person ingests sufficient quantities of high quality protein and vitamins the transition to a state of chronic hepatitis will not occur.

If someone develops chronic hepatitis and the condition grows worse to the extent of turning into cirrhosis of the liver then the situation is really grave and all is lost. No matter how one clamors for doctors, medicine, injections, good protein, etc., it will be to no avail. In cirrhosis the liver becomes hard as a rock and the bile is not excreted at all. The membrane becomes thin with a whitish color and water starts to collect in the stomach.

When this happens, since there are no strategies that can be followed or positive steps that can be taken to change the situation, the sad fact of the matter is that one can only sit there and wait for death to come. The number of such deaths has grown recently and, as we mentioned in the introduction, it has become the ninth most lethal disease in Japan (seventh for males). Some doctors predict that chronic hepatitis will become the national disease of Japan in the next century, and if the present state of nutrition giving an inadequate diet continues, that very prediction may just well be confirmed. I should like to suggest that Spirulina become the "national food" to cure this "national disease".

Pain of gastritis and ulcers disappears in one month. Chlorophyll has an antiphlogistic (anti-inflammatory) effect on gastritis and gastric ulcers.

As some people know the medicine prescribed for gastritis and gastric ulcers contains chlorophyll. Since chlorophyll has the effect of curing inflammation of the mucous membrane of the stomach and bronchial tubes it is used as a medicine in the treatment of gastritis, gastric ulcers and bronchitis.

All these are illnesses that originate in the stomach and it has always been said in the past that the stomach becomes ulcerated when one indulges in excessive ingestion of alcohol or salty food.

Now, however, it seems that over eight percent of the stomach ulcers are caused by stress rather than over-indulgence.

The stomach wall secretes gastric juices which have a powerful digestive capability. These juices can dissolve any piece of meat in twenty minutes or so. Now in order to protect the stomach wall from inflammation caused by this gastric juice there is a mucous membrane. However, when people begin to worry a lot, when there are problems at home or at work, they become stressed and the stomach membrane begins to fulfill its protective function with less efficiency. The gastric juices secreted by the stomach itself begin to dissolve the stomach wall and gouge out holes or pits in it. This is gastritis or, in the severe cases, ulcers.

In recent days ulcers have been increasingly reported among even elementary school children. The direct cause seems to be the stress attendant upon the "examination-hall" system in Japanese education. (Professor Masayoshi Namiki of Asahikawa Medical School has written a report on ulcers in these children.)

Now, since chlorophyll has the capacity to redress the inflammation of the membrane and since Spirulina contains large amounts of chlorophyll, we judged that Spirulina might have some therapeutic effect if prescribed for patients suffering from gastritis and ulcers.

As far as the patients were concerned this was not a medicine and thus they ingested it without concerning themselves with a strict schedule (before or after meals, etc.) Nonetheless within a month or so the subjective symptoms of pain in the pit of the stomach and nausea generally disappeared.

Since we did not have perfect statistical controls we are not yet in a position to publish the data but, to the extent that we observed the patients to whom Spirulina. was given, we can say that the prognosis for this treatment is good.

Spirulina fulfills the missing link for those illnesses against which modern medicine is helpless

We have now looked at the therapeutic effects of Spirulina in cases of diabetes, anemia, liver disease and ulcers, and seen that these effects were far greater than anyone anticipated.

In the past 100 years modern medicine worldwide has made spectacular progress, and because of this, illnesses have come to be identified with the different organs with which they are most closely connected. This has made possible much more accurate diagnosis and treatment of a vast number of bodily ailments. But problems like diabetes and high blood pressure have not received the full benefit of modern medical advances, for they have seemingly been more or less overlooked while the attention concentrated on the more dramatic diseases. Moreover, the medicines reported about daily in the newspapers seem to be ineffective for these diseases. All in all, modern medicine seems powerless to cure diabetes and liver disease, at least to judge by the less than effective treatment which has been the norm up to now.

In the light of this and taking into account the nature of these diseases, we judged that the algae, Spirulina, might be effective in treating these illnesses because of the special character of its constituent elements. Moreover, it is a hard fact of life that the recent changes in the Japanese diet are lowering the resistance of the people to these very diseases. Thus, on the basis of our experience with the Japanese clinical situations outlined above, we should like to suggest that Spirulina become the "national food" of Japan so as to contribute to a modification of the general physical constitution of our people and thereby reverse the unfortunate, unhealthy trend of the times.

Chapter Four

EFFECTIVE IN THE PREVENTION AND TREATMENT OF HEPATITIS AND CIRRHOSIS
Spirulina—A way to save and clean the "medicine pickled" liver of the Japanese people.

by Dr. Noboru Iijima, Professor at University Hospital, St. Maryanne College of Medicine

The Liver—A biochemical factory in the body

The liver is located just below the right diaphragm and is the largest organ in the body, generally weighing about 1/40th of one's body weight, although this varies with age. From about age 20 to 60 it remains about the same size, but after that shrinks a bit. Unlike the lungs and the kidneys, there is only one liver. Moreover it is different from other organs in that it has three vascular nets (blood vessel systems), i.e., the arteries, the veins and a special third system—the portal veins. It is important to know this structure to understand the nature of liver diseases.

The portal veins are avenues of nutrition. The nutritional components absorbed from the intestines are transported by the portal to the liver where the nutrients are given to the cells of the liver. Of course there is the arterial system of the liver which supplies oxygen, but if one takes the amount of blood supplied by the arterial system to be 1 then the portal vein system's volume would be 3 to 5 times that. There is no comparison. When cirrhosis sets in, the volume of blood from the portal veins is drastically reduced and becomes about equal to that supplied by the arterial system.

There is a phrase in Japanese, "Kanjin kaname", which means "the main essential or vital point" and which employs the ideograph for the liver. This is most appropriate, for the liver is an organ for which an understanding is most essential. The liver has as many as 500 different functions which it must perform, and since most of these are based on chemical changes we are learning new things about the liver's functions constantly as the science of biochemistry progresses. Thus if the man in the street could keep in mind that there is an intrinsic relation between these functions and disease it would be a great aid in the maintenance of health. I shall attempt to explain the most important of these functions in the following sections.

Three major liver functions— synthesis and analysis, storage, detoxification

The three most important functions of the liver are probably:

1) analysis and synthesis, 2) storage, 3) detoxification. For example, the sugars (carbohydrates) which one ingests with a meal are digested by the stomach, absorbed from the intestinal tract as simple sugar like glucose and carried by the portal veins to the liver. When we take in excess sugar the absorbed glucose is further broken down by the liver into simple compounds to become the materials for the construction of protein and fats. Again it polymerizes, synthesizes the complex sugar glycogen and stores it in the liver until, when necessary, it breaks the glycogen down to glucose and supplies it to the bloodstream.

For example, when the glucose (blood sugar) level decreases because of an empty stomach, glycogen is quickly changed into glucose and dispersed in the blood. Generally the blood sugar (glucose) level is maintained at 70-100 mg.

One reason that we don't die even if we fast for 1 or 2 days is because of this activity (sugar metabolism). Thus when there is damage to the liver the metabolism of sugars does not proceed properly, the blood sugar control goes awry and a condition arises akin to that of a diabetic. One often hears cirrhosis patients complain that, "Well, I've finally gone diabetic," and this is proof of the important functions the liver performs in sugar metabolism.

Again, eggs and meat are primarily protein but when we eat these the protein is changed into amino acids through the action of enzymes in the intestines. Then these are absorbed and transported to the liver. The liver thus uses these amino acids as raw materials to make the particular proteins necessary to the structure of the human body.

I have said that the liver is the largest organ in the human body. This is important since the liver's second major function is to store those elements which are not immediately needed and to act as a warehouse for these elements, ready to supply them when needed. Among these stored elements are, in addition to the glycogen mentioned previously, large amounts of various vitamins (A, B, C, B_1, B_2, B_6, B_{12}, etc.). This is the principle reason that the liver of animals is a nutritionally superior food for us.

The third function of the liver is detoxification. In the food we eat every day there are foreign bodies, things which have a bad effect on the body, even if they are not full-fledged poisons. Somehow these must be made innocuous and the unneccesary elements must be evacuated from the body. Recently there has been concern about polluting substances, and with respect to this also the function of the liver is important.

In this manner the liver acts like a filter which takes the harmful substances from the blood and sends the pure, safe blood through the whole body.

For example when one drinks an alcoholic beverage, almost all the alcohol (90-98%) is absorbed from the stomach and intestines and is sent via the blood to the liver where it is filtered. At this point the discussion becomes a bit technical. Let us now see what the disposition of the alcohol is which has entered the liver. The first stage of the process is the breaking down of the alcohol by the activity of the alcohol dehydrogenation enzyme, upon which it becomes acetaldehyde, which is a poisonous substance. This substance is the chief cause of the hangover symptoms of queasy stomach, vomiting and headaches. In the second stage MEOS (alcohol oxidizing enzyme) acts on this poison and finally reduces it to water and carbon dioxide which are then expelled from the body. But when one drinks a large quantity the process is obstructed and this becomes a great burden for the liver.

An important point to keep in mind is the ability of the liver to dispose of alcohol, approximately 10 milliliters of alcohol per hour (1/3 oz.). This means that the liver is able to process only 3 to 3½ oz. of *sake* (Japanese rice wine) in an hour. (There does not appear to be much difference between individuals in their liver's capacity to dispose of alcohol.)

Thus if the liver is healthy as long as one drinks moderately within the bounds of these figures then drinking should not be harmful to the body. But in fact, this is not the case. Even if we talk about staying in bounds and restricting ourselves to 3 ounces or so per hour we soon go beyond that and become intoxicated.

Moreover, if one does not eat while drinking, then protein, vitamin and mineral deficiencies occur which result in the liver losing its health and which cut its function in half. When the alcohol dehydrogenation enzyme and MEOS cannot dispose of the alcohol the alcohol level in the blood rises and one becomes intoxicated.

CIRRHOSIS—The silent disease which attacks people in their prime

Well then, how does one protect the health of the liver? The answer is simple—always take in a full sufficiency of protein. Fully 70% of the liver is protein and the many enzymes which allow it to perform its chemical functions smoothly are derived from protein.

About 4% of the weight of even a healthy liver is fat, but when this proportion goes above 10% the liver swells and the liver cells grow in size, which is evidence that fat has built up in them. This condition is called "fatty liver" and occurs when excess fat accumulates in the cells because of an insufficient supply of protein. It is a disease easily contracted by those who drink a lot of alcoholic beverages without nibbling on snacks while they drink. As we mentioned previously, in order to dispose of alcohol (process alcohol) there must be simultaneously present a rich supply of protein. To insure that fat does not accumulate in the liver cells, whatever fats have not been completely burned up, if there are any, must be transported to the subcutaneous fat cells. A full supply of protein is necessary. (To be more precise what is needed is methionine, one of the amino acids which constitute protein.) Since amino acids are particularly important elements of the structure of the cells, they also help protect the liver cells from poisoning by the alcohol.

If fatty liver is not treated promptly in the early stages it will progress and change into cirrhosis. Cirrhosis is the "end of the line" of all liver diseases and is a particularly dreadful disease since, like cancer, its mortality rate, once contracted, is exceedingly high.

According to statistics provided by the Ministry of Health and Welfare cirrhosis ranked 9th among the causes of death in 1950 for the whole population. The death rate for males was higher (6th) than it was for females (10th). If one looks at these statistics broken down by age, one finds that for males between 30-40 it ranked 6th, for 45-54 it ranked 5th and for males between 55-59 it was in 4th place. Thus it is a leading cause of death for males in their prime. Cancer is indeed a dread disease with much research on a national scale being done on finding a cure for it. Because the Ministry of Health and Welfare includes all cancers under the rubric, "malignant growth", it ranks 2nd on the list of deadly diseases, but if one looks at the mortality rates for cancers of different organs one finds that only stomach cancer produces more deaths than does cirrhosis. Moreover, cirrhosis patients live years, sometimes more than 10 years, longer than cancer patients, which means that the number of people afflicted with this disease is many times the number given by the mortality figures. When one thinks about all these people suffering one is well aware of the necessity for counter measures which are national in scope. (Acute hepatitis treatment is funded by the national government.)

SPIRULINA—A source of good quality protein to save the medicine-pickled Japanese

Why have these liver diseases become more frequent? Viral infection, bad diet, excessive drinking, etc., are, of course, causes but what needs special attention here is liver damage caused by medicine. This is particularly frightening since the disease is caused by a medicine which is taken to cure a different disease. Since medicine is taken orally it is absorbed from the intestinal tract and it first passes through the liver which is thus readily subjected to this chemical onslaught. In fact there are reports which claim that 40% of all liver damage is the result of damage from medicine.

It is almost a cliché to say that the Japanese like medicine, but in former times medicines did not cause liver disorders. In the case of acute illnesses people took medicine for 2 or 3 days with a week being considered an unusually long time. But with the progress of medicine, while on the one hand acute emergency illnesses came to be cured with an injection, on the other hand chronic disorders seemed to increase in frequency and these require prolonged administration of medication which result in the patients becoming "medicine-pickled". Good examples of this are high blood pressure and diabetes. Pressure suppressants have prevented strokes, lightened the load on the heart and helped the patients to live longer but the patient becomes utterly dependent on the medication since the pressure rises as soon as the medication is stopped. Given this state of affairs one cannot afford to be complacent about what is happening to our lives. We may indeed be coming to an age of 100 million liver disease patients (an age when everyone is suffering from liver disease).

Up to about 40 years ago people with bad livers were told that meats and fatty foods were harmful and the protein intake was restricted. But since the publication of the good results in cases of cirrhosis gotten by Pateck with a high protein, high calorie diet, good quality protein began to be prescribed and that method continues to the present. The idea is that because the regenerative power of the liver is prodigious much more protein than usual is required to help return the system to normalcy.

Protein is essential throughout the entire body with adults requiring a daily minimum supply of 60-70 grams while growing children require even more, i.e., 80-90 grams a day. Protein is constructed from a number of different amino acids and since the arrangement of amino acids differs in the various animal proteins it is important to eat as great a variety of protein sources such as meat, fish and eggs as possible.

However, if we look at the manuscript of Pateck, the man who first advocated this high protein, high calorie diet for cirrhosis we find that the majority of the cases he concerned himself with were cases of cirrhosis brought about by excessive alcohol consumption. Heavy drinkers in the US also seem to drink without eating much and for cirrhosis patients of this sort the high protein, high calorie diet is certainly effective since the protein is useful in repairing the liver tissue.

When ingesting protein one should also ingest vitamins. Vitamins help the activity of the enzymes and since there are a great variety of complex chemical reactions occurring in the liver it is clear that the various vitamins are needed there in abundance. Vitamin C in particular performs an important function in oxidation-reduction and is essential to the making of glycogen. Vitamin C is also important in blood coagulation.

Yet, although this essential vitamin C can be synthesized in the bodies of many animals, it cannot be naturally synthesized in the bodies of only guinea pigs, monkeys and human beings. Accordingly, human beings must have their vitamin C supplied by the food they eat. Many foods are rich in vitamin C such as celery, broccoli, spinach, bell peppers, radish greens, strawberries, mandarin oranges and lemons, but for some reason it seems that we Japanese have gradually become vegetable haters in recent times.

From this point of view, i.e., the supplying of protein and vitamins, Spirulina can be said to be an ideal nutritional food supplement. The main reason for judging Spirulina to be such an ideal food supplement is that it is nearly a mass of protein, since it has an amazing 69.5% protein content. In contrast the protein content of fish (mackerel) is only 20%, beef 19.3%, Japanese soybean 34.3%, and Chlorella 47.8%. Furthermore any high protein food ingested orally must be absorbed from the intestinal tract and in this respect also Spirulina is superior with a digestion rate of 95.1%. This is because Spirulina is multicellular with a thin membrane and is consequently easily absorbed.

Spirulina for prevention of liver disease for which no sure treatment exists

At present Spirulina is given clinically to patients recuperating from surgery and patients with damaged livers. It is unfortunate we are still in the observation stage so that the statistics have not yet been completely gathered, but insofar as we have been able to observe it appears that there has been great improvement. This is particularly so in the case of the relation between the liver and alcohol. Speaking from my own experience I have found that taking 30 tablets or so when drinking certainly at least has the effect of preventing hangovers. This is because the high quality protein in Spirulina protects the liver from alcohol poisoning.

In any case from what one clinical physician has observed the liver of most Japanese is much too tired. The reasons are those that I have discussed above but the point is that if this situation continues our livers will be done for.

It is too late after one has become ill, thus the best strategy is to take preventative measures while still healthy. This is particularly important in the case of liver disease since there is no definite method of treatment established. Even in the case of a disease as terrifying as cancer there are strategies. For example, if stomach cancer can be discovered in its early stage nearly 100% of the cases can be cured and one can see the result of this in the gradual decline in the mortality rate of this disease.

In contrast it is extremely difficult to detect liver disease in the early stages. Since there are no subjective symptoms it is often too late by the time the disease is detected.

Thus I should like to see everyone over 30 have a liver function test run twice a year. The corporate industrial group check-up concentrates on the stomach and as yet only a small percentage require liver function checks. There is no tragedy like seeing a man in his prime, his 40s or 50s, being cut down by liver disease.

In conclusion, liver disease can in great measure be prevented by protecting the liver cells themselves. This is best accomplished by the self-controlling function of the liver itself, not by relying on doctors and medicines. I have heard that in American corporations those afflicted with liver disease cannot become officers. The reason is that since liver disease is difficult to cure and has a high mortality rate and yet could have been prevented by self-control, the patient himself bears the responsibility for his having come down with the disease because of his lack of self-control. How could a person who could not even manage the state of his own health be entrusted with the management of the affairs of a corporation? This is truly a strict, harsh business environment but it is quite possible that this attitude will spread to Japan also. Thus I should like to recommend the high protein food product, Spirulina, as a supplementary means of protecting the liver.

Chapter 5

SPIRULINA ALONE OR IN FOOD FOR THE TREATMENT OF CHRONIC PANCREATITIS
Ideal food for pancreatitis, anticipation of its medicinal use.

by Minoru Tanaka
Kyoto Medical College

The Pancreas—source of supply
for hormones and digestive enzymes

Many people may not at first understand the term "pancreatitis", and for this reason I think it would be best to begin this discussion with a simple outline of the structure and functions of the pancreas itself before moving on to the disease.

Although it is no longer the case, in former times the ordinary person was not even aware of the existence of an organ called the pancreas. It was not even included in the Asian Medicinal lists of the five organs and six viscera.

As to the location of the pancreas, it is in the deepest recesses of the abdominal cavity, and if one looks at the abdomen from the front it lies behind the stomach and in front of the spine. Around it are the duodenum, the large intestine and the mesenteric vessel net, and others. In form it is like a tadpole with the head of the pancreas where the head of the tadpole would be and the tail of the pancreas corresponding to the tail of the tadpole. The central portion is called the body of the pancreas. About in the center of the pancreas and running its length is the pancreatic duct which joins with the ductus communis choledochis, along which flows the bile, and opens into the duodenum.

The pancreas has two important functions. One is to transport the hormones insulin and glucagon, which regulate blood sugar, into the bloodstream, "the internal secretion function." Insulin is the hormone which raises blood sugar levels. The insulin is secreted by a group of cells about 1 mm. in diameter called the Islets of Langerhans and controls the amount of sugar in the blood.

The other primary activity is called the "external secretion function" where the alkaline pancreatic fluid which contains various digestive hormones passes through the pancreatic duct to be discharged into the duodenum. What we have eaten is digested in the stomach and duodenum, but digestion would not occur without the presence of digestive enzymes. The pancreas might well be called the storehouse of digestive hormones and it helps in the work of digesting food by sending to the duodenum seven kinds of digestive hormones which digest the big three of nutrition, i.e., protein, fats, sugars. These hormones include trypsin, which breaks down protein.

Thus the pancreas performs an indispensible function for us; it is the source of supply for hormones and digestive enzymes.

Pancreatitis—difficult for the amateur to detect

One of the diseases of the pancreas is pancreatitis. To give a textbook explanation, "pancreatitis is an inflammation of the pancreas which is in a state of self-digestion by the pancreatic fluids which contain various digestive enzymes." This needs to be explicated in somewhat simpler terms and such an explanation might go something like the following.

Inflammation is popularly conceived of as being brought about by some pathogen such as bacteria or a virus but pancreatitis is not occasioned by some specific pathogen. Usually the pancreatic fluid has its digestive function suppressed until it reaches the duodenum where it begins to manifest that function; this is called the activation of the hormones. However, through some abnormal turning point it sometimes happens that the pancreatic fluid is activated before reaching the duodenum or that the fluid which has been activated after discharge into the duodenum flows back into the pancreatic duct. When this happens the pancreas itself, since it is constituted of protein and fats, is digested or damaged by the digestive enzymes of its own fluid (trypsin and phosphorylase A are thought to be most important here.) In other words it begins to digest itself or to self-destruct. This is the basic form of pancreatitis.

As for the "some abnormal turning point", i.e., the cause of the malfunction, there are many things we do not yet understand but we can give some of the more common causes such as gallstones, heavy drinking, excessive intake of food (especially fatty foods) and the like. When gallstones get trapped in the pancreatic duct or excessive food/alcohol intake causes an abnormally high secretion of pancreatic fluid, the pressure in the pancreatic duct rises or the bile and pancreatic fluid flow back into the pancreatic duct. Consequently the pancreatic fluid is activated and the self-digestion by the pancreatic fluid is brought about.

Let us now look at the symptoms. Generally they can be divided into three kinds.

1)   Symptoms which derive from the inflammation itself.
By far the most prevalent symptom is a pain in the upper abdomen and the back. Moreover these are most often lingering and very difficult to eliminate. On occasion chills and fever can also be observed at the same time.

2)   Symptoms stemming from digestive and absorption malfunctions due to lowering of pancreatic external secretion function.
These symptoms are observed after drinking alcoholic beverages or after eating, especially fatty foods. They include nausea, vomiting, swelling of abdomen (a feeling that the upper abdomen is inflated) and diarrhea. Further there is a weight loss which occurs as these symptoms repeat.

3)   Symptoms arising from metabolic disorders (diabetes) resulting from malfunctions in the pancreatic internal secretion function.
These symptoms are similar to those which occur in the case of diabetes, i.e., parched throat, drinking large quantities of water, and heavy urination. Sometimes disorders of the peripheral nerves also make their appearance.

When these symptoms appear pancreatitis may be suspected as the underlying cause but no definite diagnosis can be made on the basis of subjective symptoms alone. Thus it is necessary to run a number of tests for reference. The principal test foci are the following:

The increase in blood serum amylase (an enzyme which breaks down sugar), although this can only be tested very early after the outbreak of the disease, the increase of amylase in the urine, the increase of white corpuscles, exacerbation of red corpuscle sedimentation. In addition, tests are made for decline in the external pancreatic secretions by testing the pancreazymin and secretin, decline in the sugar resistance factor (this indicates disorders in the internal pancreatic secretion function) through sugar load tests, and the attendant metabolic disorders such as "fatty blood". In addition there are digestion-absorption tests, pancreatic syncograms, and various radiological tests which can often detect abnormalities.

Dietary treatment is crucial for pancreatitis

As for treatment, if the cause is clearly understood it is simply a matter of eliminating it. For example if the case is cholelithiasis (gallstones) one removes the stones or if the cause is alcoholic overindulgence one prescribes abstinence from alcohol.

Dietary treatment plays an important role in the treatment of pancreatitis but on the reoccurrence of chronic hepatitis or in the acute state then fasting is considered desirable. Once the acute state has passed, the quantity of food is gradually increased. What is important at this point is that the food be easily digestible, that it be strictly well-balanced in the appropriate quantity and that it be chewed well. Naturally it is necessary to restrict fatty or spicy foods.

Now in addition there is the pharmacological aspect of the treatment. Here some of the commonly administered items are a digestive enzyme medication, a gall bladder (bile) control medication (this helps the flow of bile) as well as antibiotics to prevent secondary infection and compounds like chlorophyll A and abrocinine as antifermentators (anti-enzymes). After this, in those cases which are accompanied by diabetes there is a necessity for also administering insulin or oral diabetic medication but in this case one must be very careful because pancreatic diabetes fluctuates wildly.

Spirulina is a constitutionally well-balanced, high quality protein food with an extraordinarily high degree of digestibility. Moreover since its fat content is comparatively low and it contains a great abundance of minerals and vitamins there is hope that it will harmonize the nutrient metabolism of pancreatitis patients for whom both the internal and external pancreatic secretion functions are operating at low levels. In addition since Spirulina contains 2 to 3 times as much chlorophyll A, which inhibits trypsin, than most land plants, it is hoped that it will also be effective as an anti-enzyme medication.

We targeted the out-patients who were deemed to have light or moderate cases of chronic pancreatitis and administered Spirulina and are continuing to have good results. Because of this I should like to cite a few examples.

In 2 weeks diarrhea, and in 5 weeks nausea disappear

Case 1:   Male, 46, height 167 cm., weight 58 kg.

For about a year this patient had experienced repeated occurrences of nausea, vomiting, upper abdominal pain and diarrhea after meals while his weight decreased by 3 kg. Originally he was quite a big eater but the symptoms intensified particularly when he had ingested milk or fatty foods. He was a moderate social drinker.

At the initial examination his blood serum amylase was 173 and his urine amylase level was 386, both abnormal. His general blood-urine tests, liver function tests, protein analysis, protein fractionalization and blood sugar levels were normal. There were also no abnormalities discovered in the stomach, duodenal or gall bladder flouroscopic tests, (literally "shadow" or "contrast" tests).

The result of the examination was a diagnosis of chronic hepatitis. The treatment decided on was a dietary treatment supplemented by 21 tablets of Spirulina daily and a digestive enzyme medication. As a result, after two weeks the nausea and vomiting continued but the incidence of diarrhea decreased from once a week prior to treatment to only once in two weeks and the amylase level returned to near normal both in the blood, 160, and in the urine, 261.

At the end of five weeks both the nausea and the vomiting completely disappeared. After thirteen weeks his weight returned to his original 61 kg.

Cure after eight weeks—
combination dietary treatment and simple dosage

Case II. Male, 35, height 170 cm., weight 59 kg.

For about three months prior to treatment this patient began to experience back pain about two times a week. This would worsen when he consumed fatty foods or alcohol and would sometimes be accompanied by diarrhea. The quantity of fatty foods and alcohol did not seem to be particularly high in his daily diet.

At the time of the initial examination there was oppressive pain in the upper abdomen but the results of the various tests, i.e., blood and urine amylase, general blood urine liver function, protein fractionalization, blood sugar, were all normal. Nor was there any abnormality discovered in the stomach-duodenal or gall bladder fluoroscopic tests.

Although no abnormalities were detected in the tests, the patient was diagnosed to have a light case of chronic pancreatitis on the basis of an interview, subjective and objective symptoms. (Particularly in light cases such as this it is not always easy to detect the amylase abnormality; thus it is not infrequently the case that a diagnosis is made on the basis of interviews and both subjective and objective systems.)

As a method of treatment we started with suggestions concerning diet and simple independent dosages of 21 tablets of Spirulina per day. After the administration of the Spirulina the pain gradually abated and in three weeks there was only a feeling of pressure in the upper abdomen once a week or so. Other pains and the diarrhea completely disappeared. After eight more weeks the feeling of pressure also disappeared and his weight increased 1 kg.

It should also be tried in cases of heavy or acute pancreatitis

We have now discussed the expectation for Spirulina as an ideal food for pancreatitis patients as well as the hopes for its use as a medication, based on an awareness of its constituent structure, and we have also given a sample of its effect in actual situations.

We have reported on its effects in the case of out-patients who were judged to have light or moderate cases, but since we can expect it to be quite effective also in the case of acute pancreatitis or serious chronic pancreatitis we should now like to gather data for these more serious cases also hereafter.

Chapter Six

LOST VISION RAPIDLY RESTORED
Continuous improvement in cases of cataracts, glaucoma, etc.

by Yoshito Yamazaki, M.D.,
Lecturer, Tokyo College of Medicine and Dentistry,
Director, Kazuo Yamazaki Ophthalmic Clinic

Proverb of the new medicine:
"The eye is the mirror of the body"

A classic witticism of the Edo Period (1603-1868) says, "If one has the sensitivity (interest) the eyes say as much as the mouth." This seems to mean that between a pair of lovers it is possible to express one's feelings, wordlessly, with a glance. Indeed it would be strange to be able to express in words the inner workings of the heart.

There are also the sayings that "the eye is the window of the soul" (Confucius) or "the mirror of the soul" (Mencius), but from the standpoint of an ophthalmologist one wants to say that the eye is the mirror of the body. This actually is much more scientifically accurate.

That is because, with today's highly developed ophthalmological testing techniques one can make precise tests on the fundus of the eye, the crystalline lens (eye lens), the cornea, etc. Through these one can detect the symptoms of various diseases including hereditary diseases, high blood pressure from diabetes, hardening of the arteries, brain tumors and kidney inflammation. Thus they are important diagnostic tools.

Diet is crucial in the treatment of eye diseases also

Thus by examining the state of the eyes ophthalmology is useful in the detection of diseases throughout the body, but what about diseases specific to the eyes themselves?

In ophthalmology before the second world war, when research emphasized forms of conjunctivitis, such as trachoma (pink eye), which were epidemic diseases there was a high rate of blindness and the nucleus of the treatment was eye washes. But after the war, with the general elevation of public sanitation and the proliferation of antibiotics, the incidence of trachoma has dramatically decreased and the age of ophthalmology's strong reliance on eye washes has ended.

In contrast, however, there has been a marked increase in the incidence of eye diseases among adults and senior citizens, such as high blood pressure, cataracts, glaucoma and retinal damage caused by diabetes, as well as nearsightedness (myopia) among children and students. It is these that are the theme of modern ophthalmology. Ophthalmologists refer to this as a change from a red eye clinic to a white eye clinic.

Accordingly the central therapeutic attitude has also changed into one primarily concerned with how best to preserve vision.

Presently the incidence of chronic adult diseases such as high blood pressure and diabetes shows a tendency to increase more and more as the average life span is lengthened. This is of crucial importance for the field of ophthalmology also, since these internal diseases quite frequently induce secondary eye diseases.

As for the treatment of these eye disorders of the adult disease type, what is fundamental is to control the original ailment (basic disease) and stabilize the patient's physical condition. In order to do this one must not neglect the daily routine of the patient, i.e., diet, proper exercise and sleep.

Among these the diet, which looks like such a simple thing, is actually comparatively difficult to regulate but it is of utmost importance. It would not do to have an imbalance in the nutritional elements and thus it is necessary for the patient to carefully choose foods which are balanced nutritionally, primarily vegetable. It was because of this that I used Spirulina as a supplementary "medication" for patients with eye diseases.

Effective in 90% of geriatric cataracts (480 cases)

In October of 1976 I received a supply of Spirulina tablets from the Greater Japan Chemical Ink Industries, Inc., and have since then been using it and monitoring its effect as an adjunct to internal and local eye medication for patients with eye diseases, especially those related to "adult" diseases. These include geriatric cataracts, diabetic retinal damage (retinitis), nephritic retinal damage (retinitis), high blood pressure and hardening of retinal blood vessels (angiosclerosis).

On the basis of this use I can report that for 90% of 480 cases of geriatric cataracts the progress of the disease was arrested and/or vision was improved. Good results were also achieved in 320 cases of high blood pressure and retinal angiosclerosis. Moreover, although there are only a small number of cases, we are having spectacular results by giving 30 tablets of Spirulina a day to patients in conjunction with a combination of one or two of the following medications: adona transamine (both are hemostatic agents) and Jolethin (a wetting agent-*yueki,* electrolyte, nutriment). This combination is employed when retinal hemorrhaging is severe in cases of nephritic retinitis and diabetic retinitis.

When administering the Spirulina we first gave the patient strict orders about his/her lifestyle with special emphasis on diet. At the same time we prohibited TV viewing and suggested that the patient wear protective glasses to cut ultraviolet radiation (lenses which change intensity of color depending on the amount of light present are most desirable e.g., photo-brown, photo-grey, rapid grey, sun grey, sun brown, etc.).

For cataracts we prescribed cataract eye drops (lotion) to be used four to five times a day, usually choosing one of the following Tachion, Cineraria, Catalin, Phacolysin. In addition internal medication, such as Tachion, Parotin or Thiola, was also to be taken in prescribed dosages after meals, together with the Spirulina.

The dosage varied with the severity of the disease, i.e., light cases were given ten tablets twice a day after morning and evening meals while others took ten tablets after each of the three meals. In addition once every week or two we conducted vision tests as well as detailed laboratory tests.

As a result we were able to achieve the success referred to above, i.e., 90% of 480 cases showed improvement, and I should like to cite some of the more remarkable case histories.

72-year-old woman's cataracts cleared

Case I. Female, 72, Right eye—geriatric cataract, Left eye—
adhesive leucoma (conglutinative white spot in corner) and recur-
rent glaucoma. At the time of the initial examination (Dec. 2,
1977) her vision was: Right—0.8 (*uncorrectable*), Left—could
barely sense light.

The examination resulted in the above diagnosis and for the
method of treatment we decided to emphasize treatment of the
cataract and the glaucoma.

First, medication: For the cataract we prescribed cinelaria (a
cataract medication) to be dropped in the eye three to four times
daily. For the glaucoma in the left eye we prescribed the following:
1) Pilocarpine (drops to relieve eye pressure) to be dropped in the
eye two to three times daily, 2) Tachion (cataract inhibitor) 100
mg., 3) Parotin ("sleep liquid" gland hormone, i.e. Meibomian
gland hormone) 10 mg. Three tablets of each of these last two
were taken each day, one after each meal. After April 27, 1978
Spirulina was added to the regimen, with an average of 20 tablets a
day prescribed. She was encouraged to take as many as 30 to 40
when she felt particularly bad or was extremely tired.

This patient was a woman who faithfully followed the instruc-
tions of her doctors and particularly because her left eye was
sightless she was very much aware of the importance of her eyes.
She came to the clinic faithfully once a week without fail for the
time of the initial examination and was in all respects a model
patient.

Her diligence was gradually reflected in the results of the
treatment and now the vision in her right eye has improved to 1.5.

It may be superfluous to mention that this lady came to be
called the "Spirulina grannie" because of the PR she did for
Spirulina in the waiting room.

Complete cure of a white collar worker's difficult illness

Case II. Male, White collar worker, 33

Illness: Harada's Disease. This disease is not restricted to the eyes but is an illness of the entire body which attacks those parts of the body which have coloring matter (pigment) such as the hair, skin, inner ear and the cerebral meninges. It is an acute, pervasive inflammation of the choroid coat of both eyes and it characteristically is found in teenagers and young adults. As for symptoms, there is a swift and violent, pervasive, nonpurulent inflammation of the choroid coat, the (hard-boil like) swelling and clouding of the choroid coat becomes strong and the retina detaches. Vision is severely obstructed and this is accompanied by headaches, earringing and nausea.

At the initial examination (February 4, 1974) the patient's vision was 0.01 in the right eye and 0.02 in the left. He was immediately admitted to the hospital.

From the time prior to coming to our clinic the patient had suffered from severe congestion and dim vision (film over his eyes) and had received treatment at a different clinic. At the time he was first hospitalized in our clinic he was given medication based on a diagnosis of *uveitis*. He was thus given Orgadrone (an adrenocortical hormone) drops four times a day along with Ecolicin drops (an antibiotic of the macrolide family). We also administered each day 6 tablets of "Vitamegin" (Vitamin B Complex) and 4 tablets of 0.5 mg. Dexamethasone (a steroid). He was also given a continuous subcutaneous (hypodermic) injection of Calomide (a vitamin B12, blood-building medication) once a day as well as 100 tablets of sasaron (a low, striped bamboo which is pulverized to a powder and made into tablet form) taken orally throughout the day.

Afterwards the designation of the ailment was changed to Harada's Disease and after one month the vision in his right eye reached 0.1. (0.2 corrected) and 0.2 in his left (0.4 corrected). By October 11 the right eye was 0.9 and the left 1.2, or almost normal readings. The course of treatment went smoothly and he was finally released on November 15.

After his release he returned to the clinic as an out-patient once every three or four days for treatment, until February 1975 when the frequency was decreased to once a week. However, on December 11, 1978 both eyes became suddenly congested and a large number of static masses appeared on the rear surface of the cornea. We administered six tablets daily of both darsen (an enzyme which breaks down protein) and calomide (Vitamin B12 and blood building medication), but the K-P (static masses behind the cornea) did not quickly or satisfactorily disappear. Even though his vision was still about 0.9 he kept complaining that things appeared blurry or filmy.

Thus on January 7, 1979 we began giving him 30 to 40 tablets of Spirulina in combination with calomide and sasaron. At a detailed examination conducted on March 18 it was found that the K-P had nearly disappeared and by April 15 they were completely gone. The patient now has absolutely no problem with blurred vision.

Complete recovery from diabetes—obesity conquered

Case III. Female, Office worker, 29
    Ailment: Diabetes, pseudo-myopia and asthenopia (eyestrain)
At the initial examination (Oct. 30, 1975) her vision was: right eye 0.7, left eye 0.9.

This patient had contracted diabetes when she was in the sixth grade and had been receiving treatment at another clinic. She was referred to us by her primary physician who thought it would be best for her to have her eyes examined. She was a very heavy person with a urine sugar level of plus 3 (extremely high), urine protein was minus (negative) and blood sugar level over 250.

Tests on the fundus of the eye revealed, possibly because of her youth, that the veins and arteries were almost normal and there were no hemorrhage spots or varicosity to be found. Varicosity occurs when the veins expand and swell to make a random snake-path pattern. Varicose veins are most often seen on the calf and are quite common in females who have been pregnant often.

Since there was no cloudiness in the crystalline lens, we judged that the diabetes itself, being only of this degree, could be completely cured by a solution of mezo-tartaric acid calcium (This is a medication developed by Dr. Fumimasa Yanagizawa of the Yanagizawa Adult Disease Research Center in Shibuya, Tokyo, and sold under the trade name Yanatōl lit. yanatōru). Since we also judged that precise information about dietary treatment of diabetes was necessary we referred the patient to a specialist in diabetes treatment, this same Dr. Yanagizawa.

For the eye ailment we decided to prescribe drops of Ecolicin (an antibiotic) and Sancoba (eyestrain medication) as well as one or two drops of Mydrin (a mydriatic or pupil dilator) at bedtime. We decided to monitor the progress of the treatment by tests conducted once a week.

By November 20 vision in both left and right eyes had become 1.5 and the pseudo-myopia had improved to a state of normal vision. In addition the other peculiar symptoms of diabetes of which she had complained, such as the heaviness in the occipital region (back of the head), the listlessness of the body, and parched mouth were almost completely gone. Her general physical condition was greatly improved.

Since we received a supply of Spirulina at that time we decided to prescribe that from Feb. 18 she take 30 tablets daily spread throughout the day and she has continued to do so up to the present time. As a result the urine sugar results are minus (negative) and the blood sugar has returned to normal. Moreover, her body became streamlined. Looking at this beautiful young lady one found it hard to believe that she was once that obese patient we met at the day of the first examination.

Recovery from retinal hemorrhaging in one month

Case IV. Male, College Student, 23

Ailment: Severe myopia in both eyes. Hemorrhaging in right retina.

In February 1953 at the medical examination given when he started school his vision was only 0.03 in both eyes and even after correction did not get better than 0.08. Because of this it was even suggested that he attend a special school for the blind. Both parents were naturally concerned and brought him to the clinic where I first met him.

At that time there were only hard contact lenses, not soft ones, but the lenses were ordered and fitted as soon as possible. His vision improved far beyond expectations and now he wears soft contacts, maintaining a level of vision in both left and right eyes of 1.0 to 1.2.

This patient is presently a senior in engineering and does quite a bit of drafting. Even before he entered college I repeatedly warned him to avoid any field which would be likely to be extremely hard on his eyes. Be that as it may, starting to do things like drafting as part of his studies in the engineering school was not a good idea.

As might have been expected, on Jan. 28, 1979, while he was a junior, he came to this clinic, worried because the vision in his right eye had suddenly weakened considerably. We thus conducted detailed tests and discovered small hemorrhage spots at the yellow spot of the right retina.

We informed the patient of this diagnosis, ordered complete rest for him and commenced treatment.

The medication for the treatment consisted of 6 tablets of Adona (a hemostatic), 6 tablets of Jolethin (an iodine product), 3 tablets of Transamin (a hemostatic), with the daily dosage being given together in three doses. At the same time we administered repeated injections of 10 mg. of *Kaytwo* (a hemostatic injection) along with 30 tablets of Spirulina daily.

Whereupon the hemorrhage spots were quickly absorbed (quickly faded) and his vision improved so rapidly that after a month his vision had returned to normal, 1.0 with contact lenses. He is continuing to take Spirulina even now.

Case V. Male, Office worker, 29
Ailment: Severe myopic astigmatism of both eyes. Unequal (irregular) visual *uveitis* and a cataract of the right eye. At the time of the initial examination (June 24, 1978) his vision was 0.05 right and 0.1 left.

This patient had had blurred vision in his right eye for two or three years prior to his coming to the clinic and had been receiving treatment for this from an ophthalmologist in his neighborhood, but since there had been no improvement he came to us. The results of detailed tests revealed that he had severe congestion of both eyes (bloodshot) and we discovered static objects on the rear surface of the cornea (K-P). His vision, even with glasses, was only 0.3 and his head ached to such an extent that he couldn't work.

As medication we prescribed Ecolicin—(an antibiotic) and Flumetholon together in eye drops, as well as drops of *tation* (a cataract inhibitor). Also we directed him to orally take 2 tablets of Taazen (an antiphlogistic enzyme medication).

Since there was no improvement in the uveitis symptoms, due perhaps to the fact that he only received treatment once a week as an outpatient, on November 19 we prescribed that he start taking 30 tablets each of Spirulina and sasaron daily spread throughout the day. Twenty days or so after he started taking these, both the congestion (bloodshot condition) and the K-P were almost completely cleared up and his vision, with glasses, improved substantially to 0.8 for the right eye and 0.7 for the left. With contact lenses he was able to achieve a level of 1.0 in the right and 0.9 in the left eye. In this way when, due to a cataract in one eye only, the degree of myopia is quite different for the two eyes, it is very difficult to use glasses and achieve a balance. Fitting the patient with contact lenses in such a case is a great convenience.

Effects on Behcet's disease and Smon's disease

We have now looked at five case histories, but in addition to these cases it would seem that merely the continuous use of Spirulina by itself (not in combination with medication) can make certain eye diseases more difficult to contract. This is particularly so for people with allergy-prone constitutions, people with weak (sensitive) skin, school children with spring catarrh, and people who are prone to contract phlyctena. (This is commonly called leucoma and it consists of slightly protruding or bulging small red-yellow-white spots appearing in a circular pattern around the cornea or the globe conjunctiva, together with the surrounding portions of the conjunctivia becoming congested or bloodshot. It is commonly found in infants and adolescent girls and its cause is said to be either a tubercular allergy or fatigue of the whole body.)

However, in order to allow Spirulina to fully demonstrate its effectiveness it is important, as I mentioned earlier, to maintain a proper lifestyle and strictly avoid between-meal snacks and odd or unbalanced foods.

Not only this, but also Spirulina has some effect when taken continuously in large doses on those diseases which are said to be intractable such as Harada's Disease, which appeared in case II, Smon's Disease, hemorrhaging of the retina vitrous body which sometimes occurs in juveniles or adults, and even on the supposedly incurable Behcet's disease.

Moreover, in the first part of June 1979 the owner of a Tokyo optical shop who frequently visits the clinic was completely cured of abdominal hemorrhaging, thought to have been brought on by stress, through a combination of rest, dietary treatment, and 30 tablets of Spirulina daily, without the use of any other medication at all. Even today he continues to take 20-30 tablets a day as a preventative measure.

With respect to the dosage of Spirulina, we used 20-30 tablets daily as a standard dosage and these are examples of patients continuing this dosage for 600 days. In no case were any side effects observed to have been caused by such prolonged use. We are confident that long-term large dosages of Spirulina can be prescribed with a feeling of security.

It goes without saying that the self-recuperative power of the individual patient for all diseases—not merely eye disease—has quite a bit to do with the speed of recovery. It is hyperbolic to state that Spirulina strengthens this self-recuperative power since it is an alkaline food which contains abundant vitamins, minerals, chlorophyll and easily digestible protein.

From the viewpoint of treatment, this then is the supplementary function of Spirulina, and from the studies we conducted we believe that there is no doubt of its having had a large positive influence on therapeutic efficacy.

Spirulina is also ideal from the perspective of nutrition. According to the literature published by people who have researched this, they were impressed by Spirulina's nutritional balance which is so good that they found it hard to believe that it could be obtained from natural vegetation. Moreover, once we used Spirulina in actual clinical situations we found that it was not a mere nutritional supplement but that it could be applied to the treatment of chronic "adult" diseases. This presents an important topic of investigation for medical research hereafter.

The therapeutic efficacy of Spirulina which I observed was quite a bit higher than I ever expected at the beginning and I should like to continue to add to the data in the future.

Chapter Seven

AMELIORATION OF GASTROPTOSIS AND ULCERS IN MY PATIENTS
Controlling modern diseases of the digestive tract occasioned by foods with artificial additives

by Dr. Tomokichi Sakai,
Internist and Physiologist
Professor, University of Eastern Japan

Aging without growing old—growing old gracefully

"Everyone wants to live a long life but no one wants to grow old." (Swift) This is certainly true.

The average life span of the Japanese has increased and the senior citizens have come to play more of a role in the overall structure of society—the arrival of the "mature society".

But like it or not sooner or later everyone grows old and ultimately dies. This is the destiny of all living beings. Thus, although there are differences of degree, there is no one who does not harbor feelings of anxiety and fear with respect to the inescapable human lot of aging and death. In other words, even though one lives many years, one does not want to become an old person. Ultimately, of course, this is only wishful thinking and reality is not so accommodating. Nevertheless we still do not clearly understand why it is that we must age and die. In fact it is precisely because we do not understand the reasons for this that, all throughout our lives up to the day we die, we make all sorts of efforts to preserve health, remain young and prevent aging.

Merely jumping on the bandwagon will not make one healthy

Well then, what can one say about health? Certainly it is a fact that knowledge of medicine and medical treatment has increased and that concern for health has grown substantially in recent times. Yet from the viewpoint of a doctor who is involved in first order diagnosis and treatment, it seems as though there are still a great many people who think health is a commodity that can be purchased with money. What these people have in common, when one talks with them, is an attitude which views health as nothing more than a kind of "boom" or fad.

For example, there was a time just after the second world war when the word "culture" was so popular that it was applied to anyone and everything. Thus one heard references to "culture knives", "culture cleavers", "culture cooking pots", "culture homes", "cultured people" and even "the weekly magazine culture" and "the propane gas culture". Now it seems that the word "culture" (bunka) has been supplanted by "health" as the predominant meaningless cliché-maker. Everything is now a "health product".

Immediately terms like "health method", "health utensils", "health gym", "health center", and "health magazine" spring to mind but all of these are nothing more than faddish manifestations of something intended to meet the needs of modern people who long to be healthy.

Because of this temporary boom there are many people who take all sorts of activities to be healthy when in fact they are not conducive to good health and may even be harmful.

What I should like to have people realize from the outset is that health is something that each individual must obtain and maintain by themselves and that this is a process which requires attention over a long period of time.

On this point, I can't help thinking that the Japanese are prone to act on the basis of simplistic and single-minded thinking. If someone says that some unknown plant is good for the health then immediately there is a "boom" and that plant is "in", or if someone remarks that running is good for one's health then everyone, including the pet cat, starts jogging. And, as one might expect, this results in a number of heart attacks, and even death, because people jump into a strenuous exercise program without proper thought and planning.

When human beings do not exercise sufficiently, their body tone and organ functions deteriorate. To prevent this or restore the body to its proper level of efficiency, "doing a little exercise" will not be of much help. Unless that exercise is solidly established as part of one's daily life, if it does not emerge naturally and continuously, one will not achieve the desired end. Thus if, without respect to age or condition, everyone just starts running it is quite obvious that there will be some tragedies. What has to be made clear is that there is an appropriate exercise specific to each individual, i.e., there is no single exercise which is universally suited to all people.

Modern man enjoys the fruits of civilization in the affluence, convenience and pleasures of his lifestyle, but at the same time it is an indisputable fact that civilization has, little by little, in imperceptible increments, gnawed away at his health and created an environment and conditions which threaten human existence itself. Let us consider this point in more detail.

Problems with modern Japanese as domesticated hunters

There are many theories about the origins of the Japanese people and there is much about which we are not certain. There is, however, agreement among the scholars that for some millenia after 7,000 or 8,000 B.C., during the Jomon period, the inhabitants of the Japanese archipelago were a hunting and gathering society which sought out animals, fish and shellfish. With the coming of the Yayoi period (3rd century B.C. to 3rd century A.D.), due to influences from the Asiatic mainland, the people moved in the direction of our agricultural society centered on wetland rice cultivation.

If one compares the basic body type of a hunting and gathering people with that of an agricultural people, one finds that the agricultural people tend to have short legs and a long torso while the hunters tend to have long, strong legs and well-developed muscles since they are forced to climb about the hills, challenge the rough sea and do battle with animals. Seizing on this concept of a people's body type, Professor Isao Harada, who graduated some time before me from the University of Northern Japan and who is well-known as an aeronautical physiologist—he is presently director of the Experimental Aviation Medical Laboratory of the Self-Defense Forces—published an essay entitled, "An Alternate Theory of the Origins of the Japanese" in the Air Self Defense Forces organ *Aviation and Safety* (Hiko to Anzen: January 1978) which contains some very interesting observations.

He notes that there is very little in the way of wasted or left-over food from the officers' mess which has a relatively large percentage of older men, whereas from the predominantly young enlisted man's mess there are enough left-overs every day to keep a good number of pigs happy and content. This seems due to the older men not being able to forget the chronic feeling of starvation they felt during the second world war, whereas the young men were raised amidst an abundance of food and have not had to experience extreme hunger. Moreover they seem to think that food is the nice things that mama brings when one makes a fuss in front of her, that food is something which just simply appears when one wants it.

Today's young people have longer legs than they did in the past but it is only in their body shape that they resemble the hunting peoples, for when it comes to finding food they merely lie around and order it rather than scrambling around the fields and hills to get it for themselves. It is these modern young people that Professor Harada calls "Domesticated Hunters" or Indoor Hunters, Armchair Hunters, etc.

Because of a lack of exercise and excessive calorie intake it is only natural that these armchair hunters should become physically overweight and obese. But if one considers them in terms of actual physical strength their appearance is deceptive, for their bones are weak and will break much more easily than they should. How are they mentally or spiritually? They claim that only their ideas are correct or worthwhile and show no inclination whatever to listen to the opinions of others. Thus when they are suddenly thrust in among strangers there begins to appear a cluster of symptoms of complete maladjustment, they may contract ulcers or become misanthropic and even commit suicide. In any case they lack spiritual stamina and social adaptability.

One cannot ignore these observations of Dr. Kuroda in the clinical situation either. Modern people don't exercise their bodies, they eat what they want and only what they want and when they step out into the world there are a myriad stimuli which influence their cupidity. In addition there are all the worries, dissatisfaction, disappointment and expectations involved in ever more complicated social and personal relations.

Processed foods and refrigerated drinks
that threaten your health

This then brings us to the question, "In concrete terms, how does one maintain and improve one's health in this modern society which places excessive stress on both one's body and one's mind?" In the actual clinical situation this stress may be reflected in the recent changes that have occurred in the types of digestive illnesses which are most common.

A good example of this is the many cases of gastric or duodenal ulcers in children which one encounters in clinics today where they were all but unknown in the past. The same is true of the rapid escalation of the incidence of ulcerated colitis (inflammation of the large intestine) in teens and young adults. The increase is particularly violent in the case of the colonic form of ulcerated colitis which is common in young people. In order to develop a strategy for dealing with these new forms of illness we must consider the question of the nutritional excess which has been brought about by the affluence of a modern civilized society together with what is really the other side of the same coin, namely the problems of unbalanced diet and malnutrition. That is, we must consider this a question of the disease of affluence.

Health and diet obviously have an important connection with each other and if I were to give a list of the dietary problems common to most of my patients it would be something like the following:

1. Most still use too much salt. Salty flavor is a carryover from the taste of the Meiji (1868-1912) and Taisho (1912-26) periods and has been added as an embellishment to new food products also.

2. Insufficient consumption of protein. In particular there is no balance with other nutritive minerals and vitamins.

3. A high percentage of the food used is processed food. They even go so far as to buy "brand name" pickled vegetables with

consequent loss of individual taste. In short, economy and convenience take precedence over home made flavor. This implies an escalation to stronger, less subtle flavor.

4.   Heavy consumption of confections and cold drinks. There is still a strong tendency to think "It's best to eat something sweet when you're tired," and this is evidence that we are often ruled by cravings and sensual treats.

5.   Low consumption of fresh fruit, green and yellow vegetables. In fact there is a strong tendency to dislike these foods.

Of these five the ones which have the greatest effect on health are, I think, 3, 4, and 5. With processed foods, especially instant food products, nutrition and the balance of nutritional elements play a poor second to flavor. They seem to be made so that they are very tasty and quite convenient but there doesn't seem to be any consideration given to the amount of protein or sodium they contain. The total yearly sales for instant food products is over 500 billion yen (2 billion dollars at 250 to 1) and 70% of this is consumed by young people in their teens and twenties. I must say that this is not unrelated to the large and growing number of youngsters who are weak, overweight and prone to broken bones.

Further, when stress and an unbalanced diet occur together very strange symptoms begin to manifest themselves. The human body is so constructed that when stress is very great and/or continues for a long time sodium is taken in while the calcium in the cells is expelled. What will happen, do you think, if, in a society which is very stressful at the best of times, one continues to eat as much highly salted or highly sugared food as one wants? Surely it is clear that the body's defense mechanisms will be greatly weakened.

The patients I have examined can roughly be divided into four groups according to their symptoms: 1) Cardiovascular problems, 2) Gastroenteric problems, 3) Weariness or fatigue, 4) A combination of these. Among the young people males are slightly in the majority while middle age females somewhat outnumber the males. There seem to be only a few older people but there are some who are admitted with a near blockage of the intestinal tract immediately upon eating a confection.

Spirulina helps alleviate urban dwellers' gastroenteric disorders

Let me illustrate my point with a few examples.
Case I. Male, 19, Waiter

This patient came to the clinic complaining that his stomach would start to hurt every time he drank juice, so much so that he would clutch his abdomen and double up. He said he felt as if he were being stabbed in the pit of the stomach. After various tests were performed it was determined that there was a moderate amount of sugar in his urine, some abnormalities in his electro-cardiagram and symptoms of anemia.

Looking at this patient's lifestyle and diet we found that he slept every day until noon and then would watch TV while drinking juice. He would then eat a meal of miso (bean paste) soup, pickles and rice at around 5:00, after which he would go to his job as a waiter. After work at 1:00 a.m. he would come home and fix himself a bowl of instant noodles before going to bed. This pattern had continued for a full two years. He was drinking 2 medium size bottles a day.

Case II. Female, 24, Office worker

This patient came to the clinic complaining of nausea, dizziness and itchy skin. As might be expected, her diet was not very good. She might or might not eat breakfast, for lunch she would have a sandwich or sweet bean paste buns and when she got home in the evening she would eat only a little. In addition every day she would drink 5 or 6 bottles (medium size) of cola and 7 cups of coffee (each with ½ spoon of sugar).

Case III. Male, 62, Unemployed

The patient had gotten involved in an altercation after 2 sweet bean paste rice cakes after lunch and he came to the clinic complaining of stomach-ache and constipation. An examination revealed a blocked colon and he was admitted to the hospital. His usual dietary pattern was to have highly salted snacks while drinking rice wine (sake), eat only a small amount of light foods for meals and consume almost no fresh fruit or vegetables. It would be strange if something did not go physically awry with someone who continued on such a diet for any length of time. There were many other patients who exhibited similar symptoms and if one were to include the light cases and those who displayed no symptoms but were on the verge of becoming ill there would not be enough time to enumerate.

Moreover, the sad thing is that with most of these cases it is extremely difficult to improve such imbalanced diets when they are deeply rooted and it seems often that although they may change for a short time they soon revert to their former unhealthy pattern. Habits, once formed, are indeed frighteningly powerful and changing them is a prodigious task which often gives rise to despair.

At this point I should like to interject a comment. Our present society is rapidly moving toward one in which the nuclear family is the norm, and particularly in urban centers there is an increasing number of young people living alone. In their daily life they naturally place a premium on convenience and ease, and this pattern tends to become habitual. There simply is very little opportunity for them to reflect on their eating habits, evaluate them or compare them with others.

Parental ignorance of nutrition is frightening

Rather than this sort of situation, what I am most concerned with is the huge number of mothers who are good at being women but are not so adept at being mothers. In recent days diabetes is not all that rare in children but if one asks the mothers of overweight children who have that kind of disease about the content of the child's diet it is clear that the diet is unbalanced. If one looks at the National (Citizens') Nutrition Survey conducted by the Ministry of Health and Welfare one finds that the Ministry points out that the people in general are overweight, lacking in physical strength and tend to consume too much refrigerated liquids. No matter how carefully the people are instructed to change their unhealthy eating habits this is not translated into action in the daily life of the people. There are times when we simply tell a mother that she is the cause of her child's disease. Nonetheless there are many young mothers who make no attempt to change the dietary pattern.

It is frightening for a physician to think that these children, raised in an environment which emphasizes instant and ready made foods and whose tastes have become habituated to this, will soon grow up to form nuclear families and pass along their tastes. These days the mass media in Japan are discussing the way we will live in the 80s from all sorts of perspectives but as far as I can tell there hasn't been anyone who has analyzed the effect our present dietary habits will have on the next generation.

To return to the main point, if mothers think that giving the child whatever processed food or confection he or she desires is being kind they are making a great mistake. To do this is nothing more than conditioning them to be both physically and mentally weak. It may even be said to be a crime perpetrated on these children. The same considerations apply, of course, to the father also for there are many men in Japan today who may be successful as males but are not as fathers.

Qualities of Spirulina which the modern world needs

Given these conditions we need some alternative strategy so that somehow or other we can avoid illness and maintain health. To this end we must ingest large quantities of balanced protein, vitamins and minerals. I shall leave the detailed discussions of Spirulina's composition to Professor Nakamura elsewhere in this volume and shall here only touch on a few of Spirulina's nutritional strong points.

1.   High percentage of protein with good distribution of necessary amino acids. Easily digestible also.

2. Contains large amounts of potassium and vitamins.

3. It is a nonprocessed (no additives) alkaline food product.

4. Large amount of natural colorants. Hope for medicinal applications.

Nutritionally superior protein is indispensable in treating any injury, and particularly so in cases of liver diseases where good quality protein is as essential as vitamins. The benefits of large amounts of potassium will be easily understood in the light of our discussion of the problems of stress. The pharmacological activity of natural colorants is an area which still needs to be researched thoroughly but when one considers the preferred medication for treating gastric ulcers, mesafirine (an anti-ulcerant-ulcer inhibitor) is green in color and contains chlorophyllin, one can also expect Spirulina to possibly be of great service in this area.

As a result of my having implemented considerations such as this by actually prescribing Spirulina for patients I have become more and more convinced that my judgment was correct. For example, giving fresh vegetable juice and 15 to 20 Spirulina tablets a day to hepatitis patients has resulted in the rapid disappearance of both subjective and objective symptoms. Moreover, patients with other symptoms as well who have been given Spirulina recover more rapidly than do patients who have not used it. Further, when Spirulina, with its high protein content, was used (5 tablets, three times a day with meals) by patients suffering from gastritis so that the secretion of stomach acid was causing heartburn, in all 5 cases the stomach pains and discomfort disappeared.

It goes without saying that more data about how Spirulina contributes to the well-being of a variety of patients is necessary and that the research must be systematic. However, with any disease the basis of a cure or treatment is to remove those conditions which caused or would worsen the disease, to cut the disease at the roots and heighten the natural curative powers that the body itself has. Spirulina here exhibits its enormous power to maintain and promote health.

In conclusion I should like to present two letters from patients (so they can tell you in their own words about their experience).

Two cases of rapid recovery from ulcers and gastroptosis

"I had suffered from gastric ulcers for a very long time, visiting the hospital repeatedly and even resorting to Chinese herb medicine. Each day I tried to be careful of my diet and eat only those things which were easily digestible but nothing seemed to help and both the stomach pain and the constipation became increasingly worse. At that time I began to take Spirulina at the doctor's direction (3 dosages of 6 tablets each) and the illness started to get better. I shall look back at the diary I began when I started the Spirulina and shall mention some steps in the process of my recovery.

"The diary during the second week of medication refers to the new ease with which my bowels moved and the change from a stabbing pain to a steadier, tingling pain. After three weeks the stomach pains subsided, my bowels moved freely, my physical condition improved, etc. The effects of taking the Spirulina showed in all sorts of ways. Although there is no marked increase in my body weight as yet I shall continue to take the Spirulina and hope that I do put on weight hereafter."

Mr. H. S., Shitsuran City, 38, Public Employee

"I have been commuting to hospitals because of gastroptosis for twenty years and five years because of ulcers. On June 30, 1979 I had myself examined because of the intense pain I felt, received a diagnosis of a reoccurence of gastric ulcers and was given injections and medication to relieve the problem. But after ten days the sharp pains remained as intense as ever. At that time Spirulina was suggested to me as a supplement so I took 3 daily doses of 8 tablets each while continuing to take the ulcer medication. In two or three days the constipation which had plagued me for years was relieved and now my stomach has gotten much better so that I can eat without worrying. My body weight continues to increase also."   A. A., Shitsuran City, 47, Housewife

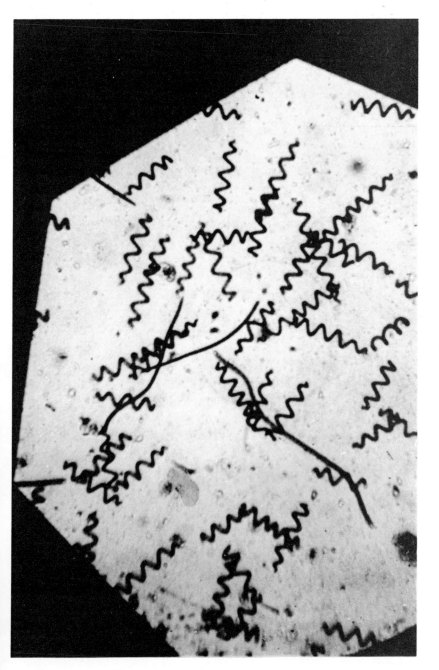

Looking through the microscope we see the cells of Spirulina moving. They can join together in filaments so close that it is hard to see the single cells.

A microscope picture of Spirulina platensis taken from a culture tank looks like a mass of wide
open spirals.

Chapter Eight

A REPORT OF SUCCESS WITH GETTING BACK LOST HAIR (CIRCULAR DEPILATION) BY INGESTION OF SPIRULINA
Only one case, but the depilatory progress was halted and the downy hair darkened.

by Dr. Iwao Tanabe, Psychiatrist and Internist (specialty in Oriental Medicine)
Denen chofu Clinic

The cause of hair loss is unknown and it is difficult to treat

Among the symptoms of depilation, the one disease which is most often observed is circular depilation (circular baldness) in which the head becomes bald starting with a round spot. As for its causes, there are many theories to account for it, e.g., instability of the autonomic nervous system, malfunction in the thyroid gland or other internal secretions, the allergy theory, abnormalities in local blood vessels, poisonings, etc., but in fact we don't as yet know the precise details of the genesis of this disease. Much importance is placed on understanding the relationship between baldness and mental or emotional influences as well as vitamin deficiencies, i.e., the relation of nutrition to depilation. Usually there are no subjective symptoms. There are some people who complain of itching scalp but the majority first notice it when it is pointed out to them by family or friends.

As for treatment, there are a number of options such as ultraviolet radiation, an external medication which causes the blood vessels in the depilatory zone to expand, and local injections. Recently there has been some success with adrenocortical hormones (steroids). There are both steroid medications for external use such as betnobate cream, linderon VG cream, full coat cream, Sephacartine which are in general use. One must be careful, however, for the prolonged use of large doses of steroids in severe cases of circular depilation results in the emergence of side effects.

An example of marked improvement

I am only going to give the example of a single case but it shows the great improvement that can be made by taking Spirulina in cases of circular depilation which has heretofore not yielded to treatment. The patient, a 64 year-old shop keeper, came to the clinic in April, 1979. He had six baldspots on his head, each the size of his thumb and separated from each other by normal hair, like the paths between rice fields. Symptomatically this was a classic example of circular depilation.

As a treatment we decided to use ultraviolet radiation, Opi-soate for local injection, and Farolisin as an external medication. After this we gave him 30 mg. of sepharantin and glitchlon daily for steroid medication. There was no effect whatever. We then have him 6 tablets of Spirulina daily since we knew that Spirulina was a high protein substance rich in chlorophyll which did not have any side effects. The Spirulina dosage started in his second month of coming to the hospital and the disease was halted in a week. Up to this time hair would fall out if he merely touched his head but now he was not losing any at all. By the second week the downy hair in the bald spots began to darken. We were quite surprised by this darkening effect on the downy hair. In those places where the baldness was complete and there was no down, however, there was no growth of new hair.

Observing the results of this treatment it seems that Spirulina checks the spread of falling hair, encourages the growth of downy hair and even acts to darken white hair. We don't completely understand why this is so but from the results of this treatment it would be reasonable to hypothesize that the Spirulina supplies nutrients to the hair and somehow acts to increase the melanin (hair contains a coloring agent called melanin which causes it to appear black). Although this was only one example I thought it deserved to be reported because of the pronounced effects.

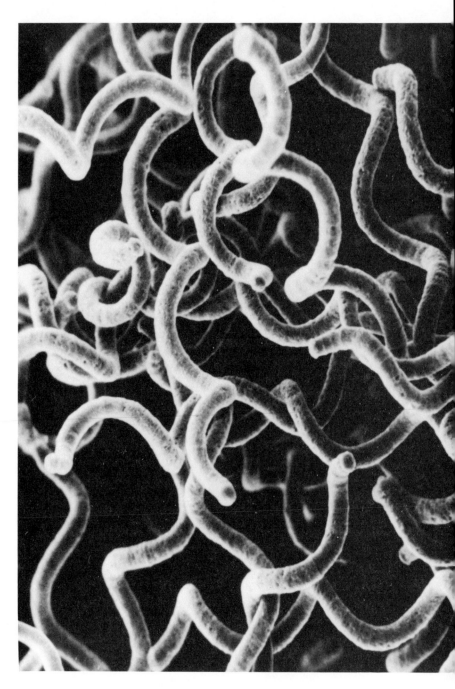

Spirulina comes in 8 or 9 different forms, all with different names such as Spirulina platensis, Spirulina maxima, etc. Sometimes the spiral is tightly wound. Here is a picture of an open Spirulina cell culture. All the different cultures can be made to unwind in filaments or open up by changing the conditions, pH, nutrients, etc., so we may be dealing with only one species.

PART III

SPIRULINA: A SAFE FOOD
An account of the thoroughgoing basic research on its safety.

Chapter Nine

SAFETY AND CHECKING IS OF PRIMARY CONCERN IN HEALTH FOODS
Pharmaceutical research on the safety of Spirulina.

by Dr. Kenichi Akatsuka, Ph.D., M.Sc.
Professor, Pharmaceutical University College of Meiji

The first condition of health food
is that it be nonhazardous and safe

For the past few years there has been a quiet boom in so-called health foods. There are probably numerous reasons for this but I should like to consider a few of the more important.

The first reason most often given is that the average life span of the Japanese has been dramatically extended with a resultant increase in the number of older people. These people have come to place great hopes in health foods as a means to fulfill their desire "to remain healthy and active."

The second is indicated by the popular saying "Modern people are always tired." Office workers, executives and others want "to get rid of that tired feeling" and seek in health foods a means of restoring their vitality. Thus we must recognize that health foods have come to play an important role in our lives. But today there are several hundred varieties of health food products being sold across the counters of the nation's shops, each claiming its own superiority. Thus the ordinary citizen, not knowing which is really best to use, simply swallows some well-worded advertisement and uses that product (simply chooses the product on the basis of the most appealing advertisement).

Of course it goes without saying that health food products are ordinarily used to "promote physical vigor, reduce fatigue and prevent illness". Thus some of the necessary conditions for any health food product are:

1. that the product be of outstanding purity

2. that it have no side effects even with prolonged use

3. that even if one mistakenly takes too much it will still not be toxic or give rise to side effects.

4. that its daily use promotes physical health and promotes the body's resistance to illness.

In the final analysis, it is only through daily use that health food products show their effectiveness. Thus, although potency or effectiveness is important it is even more important to be certain of the product's safety. How, then, does one go about testing the safety of a food product? Let us look at the actual specific case of Spirulina.

Animal experiments prove Spirulina is safe for both central and peripheral nervous system

Spirulina has almost no toxicity whatever. In order to establish Spirulina's safety pharmaceutically it was necessary to perform large scale animal experiments including tests for acute toxicity and the general pharmacological tests.

First, let us look at the acute toxicity test. Acute toxicity is expressed as one half the (minimum) lethal dosage of Spirulina ingested at one time (50% lethal dosage). We gave mice single dosages of Spirulina in the amont of 4.5 gm. for their 1 kilogram of body weight. In this experiment we found that no mice died at all. The value of the experiment lies in the translation of figures from the body weight of the mice to the body weight of humans. That is, if one traslates the 50% minimum lethal dosage for mice to that of a 50 kg. (110 lbs) human it would be 50 times that of a 1 kg. mouse or 225 gm.

Looking at this acute toxicity test, then, it is clear that as long as one does not ingest 225 gm. (approx. 8 oz.) (and this would never happen) no toxicity is exhibited. The normal daily dosage of Spirulina is only 4 gm. (from 2 to 8 500 gm. tablets) This indicates how free of toxicity Spirulina products are.

Now for the general pharmacological tests. These seek to determine what effect it will have on the organs of the body and it is through these tests that we can discover what side effect it will engender. This again is research conducted by running experiments on mice and examines in detail the central nervous system, the peripheral nervous system (heart and respiratory organs) and other organs.

First of all, the mice were fed Spirulina by mouth for a two-week period and during this time we investigated the central nervous system (brain and spine) for effects on hypnosis, anodynes (pain killers) and brain waves. The result was that Spirulina had no influence on these functions at all. In other words Spirulina did not engender any side effects in the central nervous system whatever.

Next we made a detailed examination of Spirulina's effects on the peripheral nervous system, i.e. the heart, blood pressure and respiratory system. As before, we fed Spirulina by mouth to the mice for a two-week period, checking the rate of the heart beat, respiration and administering electrocardiograms. After the mice had died, their hearts, gastrointestinal tracts, etc., were removed and meticulously examined for any adverse effects. Again, as in the previous experiment, there were no unusual effects whatever. The conclusion was that there is no danger of Spirulina giving rise to any side effects in the body's organs. Spirulina's safety was clearly confirmed by these pharmacological experiments.

What animal experiments show about food product safety

As everyone knows animal experiments are absolutely necessary to check the safety of pharmaceutical products and health food products as well. It is impossible to examine in detail the effects these substances have on each of the organs of the human body. Although not all the results of animal experiments can be said to be valid, in an unqualified sense, for human beings, nonetheless as far as tests for toxicity and development of side effects are concerned there is no better or more certain procedure, given the advanced and sophisticated research methods we have at present. On this point, it is absolutely necessary to conduct animal experiments, even if simple in design, in the case of products which are in daily use as health foods.

We have conducted this pharmacological research on Spirulina and found that it had almost no toxicity at all and that there were no side effects on the various organs of the body, from the central nervous system on. This result was gotten from the data provided by animal experiments and that data demonstrated that Spirulina was extremely safe. Remember that health food products are used to "increase the body's vigor", "relieve fatigue" or "prevent diseases" such as diabetes, liver disease and the like. Thus it is necessary to use such a product for a long time in order for it to do what is expected of it. It is because of this that, in a limited sense, the safety of such a product is even more crucial than pharmaceutical products. The experimental confirmation of Spirulina's safety was thus quite useful and rewarding.

132

Editor's Note on Photosensitivity

Chlorophyll has a tetra pyrrole structure and is a member of the porphyrin family which plays important roles in the biosynthesis of the pigments concerned with the respiration of cells, transport of electrons through membranes and carriers of charges of bioelectricity. Porphyrin is also involved in the function of oxidative enzymes which control our metabolism. In the breakdown of chlorophyll there is a biosynthetic pathway that can take the decomposition process through pheoporphyrin and pheophorbide by removing the magnesium molecule and phytol. However, this breakdown only occurs if in the process of manufacture the chlorophyll is kept for a week in the freezer and then dried instead of drying it immediately at the time of harvest.

Porphyrin compounds are highly reactive biologically and affect all the pigment systems of the human body, including the red heme of blood, especially when they are chelated with iron. Therefore the enzymatic steps identical in the biosynthesis of protoporphyrin in both plants and animals can be performed in the dark especially if glucose can be supplied as a source of energy. In a few plants such as Chlorella this reduction can occur enzymatically without light and if eaten at the precise point when the reduction is at the pheophorbide stage can cause problems with porphyrin metabolism and cause photosensitivity in humans. With fresh chlorophyll, however, this reaction does not occur and chlorophyll becomes perfectly safe. Therefore manufacture of chlorophyll products or pigments containing porphyrin must always involve prompt drying to avoid all danger and decomposition in the freezer or in the liquid state of storage in the dark. Fortunately the Spirulina made by DIC in Japan and Sosa Texcoco in Mexico, although exceedingly high in several porphyrin pigments, is dried immediately after the algae is harvested. Both being large industrial corporations they are able to avoid holding supplies of wet algae until other dryers are available. Growers of Spirulina algae are warned not to keep supplies in the refrigerator for several days and users are warned to make sure that a manufacturer's processes include quick and efficient drying. Spirulina is a natural food like lettuce or other green vegetables and will not keep, but once dried it will keep for several years in the editor's experience and probably would keep for centuries because of its ferrodoxins.

We are getting closer to the secret power of Spirulina the more we penetrate the structure of the porphyrin pigments and other biological compounds which make up all the pigments in the human body responsible for metabolism. These pigments can be found in Spirulina, chlorophyll, and human blood and are all related to the porphyrin structure. This may be the link with Spirulina's marvelous effect on the metabolic processes of the human body.

Chapter Ten

SPIRULINA SAFE FOR HYPER-PHOTOSENSITIVITY
No possibility of unexpected problems as with Chlorella.

by Dr. Koji Yamada
Associate Professor, Koriyama Women's University

Hypersensitivity to light induced by Chlorella

There are not a few proverbs and folk sayings handed down from generation to generation which have been resoundingly confirmed by modern science. Ancient man probably did not understand the world he lived in on the basis of scientific principles but in terms of an experientially developed common sense. Yet even now in the northeastern part of Honshu there is a saying which is one of those referred to above, "Feed the innards of an abalone to a cat in early spring and his ears will drop off." This is not restricted to cats, for the liver of an abalone is dangerous for human beings also. Actually, according to the records of the public health center at Ofunato in Iwate Province, there was a case of sixteen people contracting food poisoning on March 20, 1947 at Ayasato, Sanriku Village, Kesen County, Iwate Province.

Professor Michio Hashimoto of the Fisheries Department, College of Agriculture, Tokyo University, was strongly interested in this case of abalone food poisoning from the standpoint of biochemistry and food sanitation. Starting in 1960 Professor Hashimoto searched for the causal agent of this food poisoning incident and finally determined that it was a substance called pheophorbide a, which exists only in the mid-entrail glands (chu chosen) and originates in the chlorophyll of the kelp on which the abalone fed. What is most strange, it was discovered, is that this substance collects in these glands only in early spring from February to May. (For details see Professor Hashimoto's *Poisons in Fish and Shellfish,* Taub Gakkai Shuppan Center)

This is a good example of modern science validating the knowledge that ancient man had garnered from his experience. Again, it was known from ancient times in foreign lands that on rare occasions sheep or cows would eat buckwheat or St. Johnswort (Hypericum erectum) and this would give rise to symptoms of light hypersensitivity where skin exposed to light would become inflamed. It was also known experimentally that when the causal agent, pheophorbide a, or pyropheophorbide a, which are products of chlorophyll breakdown, was fed to rats it would occasion hypersensitivity to light.

However, a few years ago some daily users of Chlorella manufactured by a certain firm began to show symptoms of hypersensitivity to light with skin inflammation developing on their face and hands. A total of twenty-three victims were found throughout the country and after a study conducted by the National Institute of Hygienic Sciences, the Tokyo Bureau of Health and Tokyo Institute of Health it was determined that the causal agent of the hypersensitivity was pheophorbide *a* contained in Chlorella.*

Usually hypersensitivity is known to be caused by sulpha drugs, oral diabetic medication, antihistamines and antibiotics but it is extremely rare for food products to cause this. However pheophorbide *a*, a product of Chlorophyll breakdown, is one of those rare items and therefore it may sometimes be contained in some of the foods rich in chlorophyll, so that one must be particularly careful with these from the standpoint of food safety.

Chlorella and Spirulina are both Algae but—

What then about Spirulina? Even though Chlorella is monocellular and Spirulina is polycellular they are still both Algae. Since this was an important matter which I as a specialist in nutritional science could not ignore from the viewpoint of food hygiene, the members of our research team decided to study through animal experiments whether the pure cultured Spirulina produced by the Greater Japan Chemical Ink Industries (DIC) in Thailand, and the phycocyanine which it contained in large quantities would or would not give rise to hypersensitivity to light. The results of these experiments showed that causal agents of light hypersensitivity do not exist in Spirulina and that in the phycocyanine also there could be found no photometric activity which related to hypersensitivity. I shall thus give a report of the process by which we reached these conclusions in the space allotted to me.

Editors note: Chlorella is normally safe but this manufacturer was growing it under strange conditions which changed its character. The resulting publicity caused many people to stop eating it. Other firms had no problem but were affected by the incident.

The skin inflammation referred to as light hypersensitivity occurs through the presence of light and a causal agent. There are two basic types of reactions to hypersensitivity. In the first the entire body swells upon being bathed in light and dies some hours later. In the second type death does not occur but there do appear symptoms such as skin inflammation (dermatitis) and loss of appetite with the consequent inhibition of growth. Physiologically there is an unusual elevation in the density of potassium in the blood serum as well as in the values of the GOT activity (glutamic acid, oxylecetic acid, transaminase in the blood serum) and GPT activity (glutamic acid, pyruvic acid, transaminase), both of which are familiar from the function tests on the heart and liver.

Experimental confirmation of Spirulina's safety

In this experiment in order to determine whether Spirulina contained the causal agent for hyperphotosensitivity, we fed Spirulina to a group of white mice and raised them as well as a control group which had not been given Spirulina under the same conditions, exposing both groups to equal amounts of light. We carefully monitored change in body weight, consumption of food, the blood hematocrit level (volume of red blood cells compared to whole blood), the concentration of hemoglobin (density of red colorant), and GOT activity in the blood serum, GPT activity, concentration of sodium and potassium and the like. We also studied the photometric activity of phycocyanine on the red corpuscles.

The basic feed for the white mice was composed of 70% wheat paste (starch), 1% mixed vitamins, 4% mixed inorganic salts, 5% soybean oil, and 20% milk casein. We divided the mice into 3 groups of 10 mice each, i.e., a) the Spirulina group, b) the phycocyanine group, and c) the comparison or control group which was given neither Spirulina nor phycocyanine. In addition to the basic feed we gave the Spirulina group 10% Spirulina, and 0.5% phycocyanine to the phycocyanine group. In order to assure that the nitrogen level was the same for the control group as for the Spirulina group we gave the control group supplemental milk casein in the amount which would provide the nitrogen equivalent to the 10% Spirulina.

As I indicated previously there are two reactions to contracting hyper-photosensitivity, i.e., death or loss of appetite and inhibition of growth. The experimental data show that between the control group and the Spirulina group there was nearly no difference in terms of change of body weight, feed consumption or feed efficiency or utilization. That is to say that Spirulina does not contain the causal agent for hyper-photosensitivity.

Moreover, it is usual for the white mice which contracted hyper-photosensitivity to have increased a concentration of potassium as well as increased GOT activity and GPT activity but there were no differences to be found when the Spirulina and control groups were compared with respect to these values. This is further evidence that Spirulina does not give rise to hyper-photosensitivity. Further, when the phycocyanine group was compared to the control group there was no evidence at all to suggest that the symptoms of hyper-photosensitivity appeared in the phycocyanine group alone.

Thus we can conclude from the results of animal experiments observing the growth, feed efficiency, level of GOT activity and GPT activity in the blood serum as well as the concentration of potassium in the blood serum that there could be found absolutely no condition which would support hyper-photosensitivity either in Spirulina or in the phycocyanine which it contains. On this count Spirulina has been shown to be a safe food product which can be eaten with confidence.

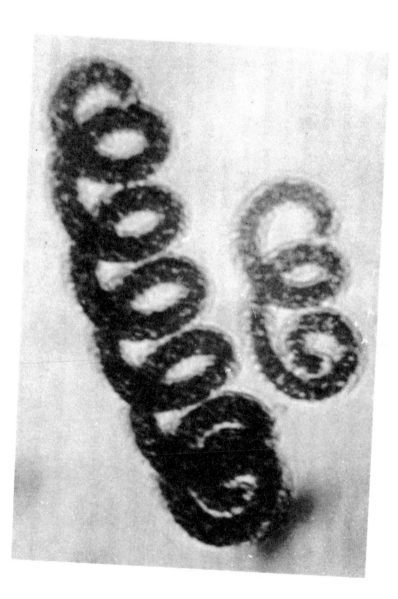

Chapter Eleven

SPIRULINA CONTAINS NO DEFORMITY-CAUSING QUALITIES.
Reports of complete safety confirmed by animal experiments.

by Dr. Yoshio Uematsu
Director, Animal Breeding Research Center

What about possible birth defects?

When a baby is about to be born everyone fervently hopes that it will be healthy and without deformities of any sort. Thus how would one react if a substance originally consumed as a food or as medication became the cause of a tragic deformation of the fetus? In Japan also the Thalidomide incident created a great stir and led to a public outcry for tightening the regulative controls (on the drug industry) to prevent drug disasters and injuries resulting from the side effects of medicines. As a perfectly natural consequence of this a general lack of confidence of medicines grew and people began to look to natural food products as an alternative to medicine. However, in such a situation it is quite easy to beat something into the ground and there are quite a few suspicious or strange food products being touted and sold as "natural foods" by unscrupulous opportunists and when this happens the products are reported widely in the mass media in a superficial manner.

Moreover, since even natural agricultural products, fish, shellfish, etc. may be contaminated by chemicals used in modern farming or by the pollutants thrown into the sea, saying that something is a natural food product is no guarantee that it is safe even when its claim to naturalness is genuine. In the case of medications, however, various strict tests are legally required to check any new product for its efficacy, safety, and its potential for causing deformities.

In the case of foodstuffs there simply is no corresponding regulative mechanism. But this is not at all to say that when it is a matter of a food product which people eat daily, absorb in their intestinal tracts and have circulated through their entire body, the question of its distribution and sale should be merely a matter of taste or preference. At least insofar as food relates to health there will come a demand, sooner or later, that it be subject to basic constituent analysis as strict as those for medicines. This is also the simple request of a nation of people who want always to be healthy.

To respond to such a request Greater Japan Chemical Ink

Industries brought the pure cultured Spirulina which they produced
in Thailand into the laboratories of the Animal Husbandry Research Institute for us to "examine Spirulina's effects on the
reproductive functions of rats and its possible effects on the next
generation." This is a report of the findings from those tests.

Detailed experiments with 80 pregnant rats

The object of the experiment was to determine whether feeding
the rats a mixture of ordinary feed and Spirulina would cause
abnormalities to occur in their reproductive capabilities so that
they could not become pregnant, or give birth to abnormal offspring if they did become pregnant. The results show that there
were no abnormalities whatever observed. The results were:

1.   Both parents and offspring developed normally and there
was no change in their general condition.

2.   There were no abnormalities in either parent or offspring
with respect to their reproductive functions. Normal offspring were
born.

3.   In the tests for deformities in the offspring also there were
no instances of deformed offspring exhibiting external deformities.

In the bone structure and inner organs tests also there were no
abnormalities or mutations which could be considered to have been
caused by Spirulina.

4.   The results obtained from the behavior and learning function tests were normal.

5.   No pathological abnormalities were observed in either
parents or offspring.

Thus the result of adding Spirulina to the ordinary feed (max-
imum 23%) was that there was no influence on the growth or
reproductive functions and no tendency to engender deformities.
Let us now discuss the methodology and scoring of the experi-

ments.

Experimental method

The rats used in the experiments were Wiestahr Imamichi rats three weeks old which were raised (preliminarily bred) for a full week after arriving at the lab and only then brought into the experiment. These rats were divided into two groups of 40 containing 20 males and 20 females each. On the basis of the feed the two groups were broken down into four categories, i.e., A, B1, B2, B3.

The A group was raised solely on the feed normally used in this lab (proportion by weight: wheat 7, corn 3, soybean husks 1.5, fish powder 1.5). This was the "basic feed" group.

The B group had Spirulina added to the basic feed and constituted the "Spirulina supplement" group. This group was further classified according to the amount of Spirulina in their food. Thus we had the B1 group (5.8) the B2 group (11.5) and the B3 group (23.0) with the numbers in parentheses referring to the percentage of Spirulina in the feed. We then compared the various B groups with the A group in a variety of test categories including pregnancy, delivery or birth, the development of newborn offspring, mobility as animals, development of intelligence, deformities and the like.

Test results—no abnormalities in bone structure or intelligence of offspring in pregnancy or birth

Throughout the entire breeding period there were no changes in the general condition of parents or offspring caused by Spirulina nor were there any deaths. The fertility test results were as follows: the males, both parents and offspring, of the Spirulina supplement group had a copulation rate of 95%-100% and the females had a pregnancy rate which ranged from 85-100%. Comparing these figures with the background data for Wiestahr-Imamichi Rats one finds they fall within the normal range.

The scores for the category of delivery (parturition) for the parents in the subcategories of length of pregnancy, number of offspring produced, sex distribution of offspring, weight of newborn offspring and death rate for newborn showed no difference between the Spirulina supplement group and the control or basic feed group. The standards for delivery and for the number surviving for at least three days after delivery were set at 79.2-83.9% and 88.6-93.2% respectively. The actual rates fell within these limits.

There was no difference between the A and B groups with respect to the death rate during the nursing period and the weaning process was normal also, as well as the sexual maturation measure (the form of the male penis, the vaginal opening and sex period cycle in females). In the various standards for the formative (structural) developmental differentiation in nursing offspring such as the ears, teeth, etc., there were also no differences among the B group.

Deformity tests

1. Caesarean section results

The rats which were the experimental subjects of Caesarean sections generally were the "grandchildren" and we performed Caesarean operations on the twenty first pregnancies and found, by comparing groups A and B and by consulting the background data on the rats used in the experiment, that in all categories of observation there was little possibility of Spirulina affecting the fetus. Further, as far as external deformities were concerned, there was one example from the A group (a lump in the meninges of the head) whereas absolutely none were observed for the B group.

2. Skeletal test results

There was only one skeletal abnormality (mutation) observed in a fetus (0.9)% and this was an asymmetry of the chest skeletal structure. No other mutations or skeletal abnormalities were discovered. With respect to the progress of the process of ossification, the second and fifth ribs were not yet differentiated in 14.8% of group B1, which must be considered high in relation to the 1.5% for group A. However, with respect to the number of coccyges and development of the metatarsal bones the B group had a higher score than did the A.

3. Internal organ test results

In addition to observing only one case (1.3)% of subcutaneous edema in group B1, there were noted cases of enlarged pelvises of the kidneys (renal pelvis) and hydroureterites (literally water-ureter illness or symptom) in group A and group B as a whole, but there was judged to be no difference in frequency between the groups.

4. Behavior and learning test results

An example of these tests is to drive a rat into a T-maze prepared so that an electric shock is administered when the rat turns left. After a number of repetitions of the same behavior the rat's behavior becomes fixed and it will always turn right even if the electric current is cut or if it is put in a different T-maze from the original. This is the behavior of a normal rat. The result of behavior and learning tests such as this did not show any disparity among the B groups nor any disparity between them and the A group.

5. Pathology test results

An autopsy was performed on all the rats participating in the experiments and there were utterly no abnormalities which could be detected with the naked eye. When the various generations were compared (A vs. B group) there were differences perceivable in weight of the organs. But none of these changes where pathological in character, and since there was no necessary connection with differences of generation or with respect to Spirulina ingestion, it was judged that these changes were not toxicologically meaningful. Thus in order to see what effect, if any, Spirulina would have on rodent reproductive functions and on the next generation, we bred rats fed on a diet of standard feed augmented with Spirulina and investigated the growth, reproductive functions, and fetal development of the next generation. The result was that there was no damage in any generation traceable to Spirulina. Thus we have come to the conclusion that Spirulina has no effect on the reproductive functions of rats and that it does not act to produce deformities.

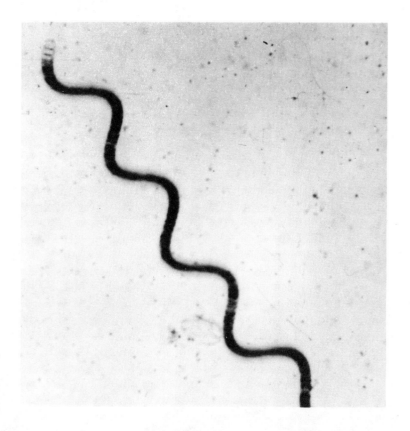

A single strand of Spirulina showing the linear development of the spiral helix.

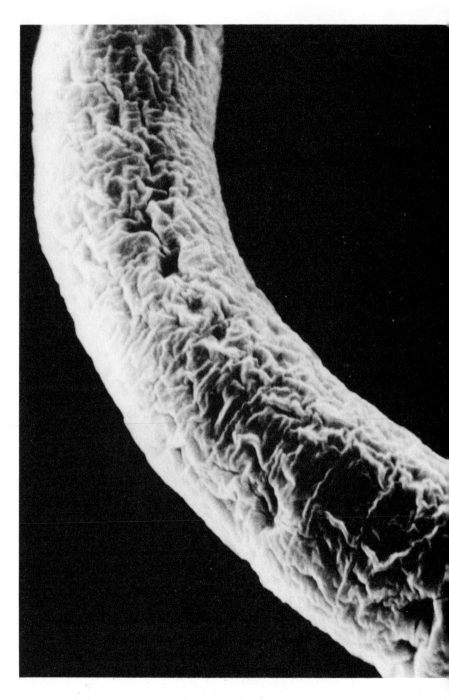

An enlargement of the Spirulina strands shown on page 126 showing the surface of the cell wall. The filaments can grow laterally in a single plane as well as lengthwise.

PART IV

A TRUE HEALTH FOOD
FOR THE MODERN AGE
Spirulina stands above the ordinary confused "health boom".

Chapter Twelve

SPIRULINA AN AID FOR OVERSTRESSED MODERNS AND THEIR IMBALANCES
Now a food in the true sense, something between a food product and a medicine.

by Dr. Naoharu Fujii, M.D.
Director, Tokyo Stress Institute

Temple records show causes of death in Japan for the past three centuries

This may be a premedical topic but a childhood friend who was kind enough to take care of my father's funeral services and who is now the chief priest of a temple once out of friendship showed me the death registry of the temple which had been kept for many centuries. This document was really a historical treasure. Although the handwriting and literary styles were diverse, the names, both secular and posthumous, of everyone who had been even slightly connected with the temple were recorded there along with their age when they died. In addition there was noted the causes of death according to the understanding of the period and the chief priest, even though it must be said that some of the causes would not be recognized as such in our modern age. Nonetheless the details were faithfully recorded here in the style of each period for three hundred years.

It goes without saying that a large number of infant boys and girls, whose precise age was unknown, were listed in the record. One unavoidable cause for this was probably the lack of medical treatment and knowledge of hygiene but in any case the high rate of infant/child mortality continued on to the nineteenth century. This was just one part of the dark veil which surrounds human life.

Next were the names of those who died when they were around twenty years old. Expressions such as *haikin* (lung metal) or *rogai* (labored or painful coughing) abound, but for the most part they would seem to refer to tubercular deaths centered on pulmonary tuberculosis. Again, when we glance through the pages we can understand deaths connected with an incident such as youngsters dying of a disease contracted on the war front some thirty years ago, or of an epidemic in the years before that or of injuries sustained in the Tokyo earthquake.

Yet in contrast to these, as we scan this 300-year registry of the end of various people's lives, what really strikes one is the notion of the innate Japanese sense of the transitoriness of things as expressed by the saying that "Human life is only fifty years long" as a fact of human existence. Up to thirty years ago or so, fifty years was the length of time an average Japanese would have lived!

The most conspicuous cause of death is stroke, or those sudden deaths which suggest stroke (cerebral apoplexy). After this come those deaths resulting from disturbances of the digestive system such as "stomach illness", "diarrhea" and the like. It would seem likely that such rubrics also covered ulcers and cancer, since there are some comments occasionally about these. In addition there are many cases of what seem to have been acute pneumonia, but this is largely by analogy. In any case, at least as far as this death registry is concerned, living to the age of seventy was a rare occurrence. A good number of those that escaped the high rate of infant mortality were pursued in their 20s by tuberculosis and the large majority of those who managed to live through that ended their lives just after passing the age of fifty. The proportion of people seventy years of age or older in a population is called the "longevity rate" and Japan is always no more than about 2.8%, although there is some sign of its being increased, compared to the American and European rate of 5%-6%. In fact, if one uses only the death registry it is questionable whether the rate ever went above 2%. In any case, this phenomenon of dying in one's fifties is quite conspicuous and it seems to have been so for quite some time. I can't help but feel that there is a connection between this fact and the fifty-five year old retirement system in Japan.

Even from the death registry of a temple, which covers a comparatively long period of time although its scope is severely limited, we can discern the changes in the life system of the Japanese connecting past with present. It can also supply a bit of concrete support for painfully felt anxieties confronting modern clinical medicine today.

One can really see that since the average life of a Japanese was terminated in this fashion until recently it was only natural that medicine should have progressed by concentrating on the various epidemic diseases and morbid alterations (acute illnesses). Such a revelation can be the basis for a restructuring of our view of the role of medical science in our present age and the hope for a new focus.

Positive means to control increased stress

At the end of February 1979 the 2nd International Stress Discussion Conference was held in Monte Carlo, Monaco in the south of France to discuss the theory of stress which has become so important to all in the past 30 years. The topic was "Stress Management", or how to live with stress.

In the Convener's Address opening the Conference, Dr. Hans Selye, Director of the International Institute for Stress in Montreal, Canada, looked forward to an ordering and consolidation of the now almost classical theory of stress as well as concrete suggestions for its application.

This theory of stress can be summarized as follows:

"The complex and subtle biophysiological functions are like a black box which permits no peeking from the outside. But for some as yet unknown reason only the portion dealing with the interaction of the interbrain, the pituitary gland and the adrenal glands allow for a glimpse. It is as if the underground waters flow out onto the surface in these areas only.

"In other words when an external pressure, or stress, is applied the pituitary and adrenal glands become an axis where the body's defensive capacity is deployed. When the body's defensive capacity is overtaxed by stress there is an outbreak of self-destructive phenomena, i.e., 1) heart or stomach hemorrhaging (ulcers), 2) enlargement of the adrenal glands, 3) contraction of the thymus gland. In this process, three stages in the emergence of real disease can be discerned: 1) alarm, 2) resistance, 3) exhaustion. When the external pressure is excessively strong there is the cessation of life activity, shock, or shock death as it might be termed. (At present this shock is considered part of medical common sense.)

"Again the human body's response to the various epidemic diseases or to unique causes, such as external injury, is identical with its response to industrial pollution, changes in the social environment or mental trauma (external); that is, the body shows resistance, then either adapts or succumbs and becomes ill. The difference in response of the body seems ultimately to be individual differences in the responders or differences in the physiological conditions operating."

Here Professor Selye's explanation turned to a somewhat bitter topic. "Stressors will change along with the times."

However, as long as there is life there will be stress and for whatever reason it seems that stress is rapidly increasing in the modern age.

It is my earnest hope that my colleagues here and our successors will publish insights and suggestions which will confirm the structure of human life wherein both mental and physical aspects function as a unity under the general rubric of stress. And from this hopefully will emerge preventative measures and treatment of various deeply interconnected illnesses as well as strategies for maintaining health and combating aging.

Further, in my own personal field of interest within the various kinds of stress, namely the mental or emotional stress which is inescapable in modern society and which becomes more prevalent as society progresses, I would hope that we could directly confront it and submit to it. In other words, to fend off stress and deal with it as happy or positive stress."

This then is a summary of Professor Selye's position.

People become ill from psychosocial stress

Over 4000 participants from 23 countries, including four Nobel Prize winners, delivered papers expressing their considered judgments and engaged in wide-ranging discussion.

For example, excluding highly specialized papers in neurophysiology, there were two viewpoints which dominated the discussions. One was stress as seen from the point of view of social psychology. Even a year before in the announcement sent to me by Professor Selye there was the following, "For whatever the reason it seems that my theory of stress is enjoying a sudden revival of interest especially in the major cities of the United States. The reasons for this seem to be, first, that there are many comparative studies of the views on stress being developed in research organizations in various countries throughout the world. Another reason for this popularity is a function of the change in the times, i.e., the viewing of stress phenomena from the perspective of social psychology."

At this conference, also, this sort of feeling was quite strong, especially among the Americans. Concentrating on the actual social situation, the reports sounded like a kind of social pathology. A summary of the main points of the discussion might be given as follows:

Here is a state of stress. When people fall into such a state and it continues for some time then many contract diseases such as high blood pressure, gastric or duodenal ulcers (particularly prevalent in the U S), heart disease, rheumatism, asthma and even neuroses and allergies. Those that already had these diseases get worse.

Now under what circumstances does one fall into such a state? The three most commonly given causes are: 1) divorce, 2) unemployment or loss of one's job, 3) forced retirement. This, then, is the theory, and if one expands divorce to include all domestic problems such as relation of wife to mother-in-law, and the schooling, occupation and marriage of the children, and if one expands unemployment to include latent unemployment, lack of fit in one's job and the anxieties of personnel factionalization then the present situation in society fits quite well in the theory. Forced old age retirement is a problem which must inevitably be addressed by all the modern industrially developed countries in the world. Dr. Stanley, the Editor in Chief (Head of the Editorial Committee) for seventeen years of the American Journal of Medicine, who was attending the conference, said to me with a preoccupied look on his face, "Even if half the participants are doctors or medical scholars the other half are psychologists, sociologists, lawyers, journalists or even dentists and veterinarians. It's really a very fascinating conference but it is completely without precedent."

When I replied, "That's quite true but from my viewpoint as a clinical physician even the grand and subtle results of DNA and RNA research (both are substances in the cells which control heredity) seem a bit like trying to repair an electric watch with a hammer and screwdriver," he smiled wryly and said irrelevantly, "My solution for stress is horse racing."

Is there no medication to conquer stress?

However, what was of particular interest for clinical physicians was the second major topic. This was a re-evaluation of ways of preventing or alleviating stress from the viewpoint of physiological structure—in other words, the simple but heartening expectation of answering in the affirmative the question, "Isn't there a medication effective against stress?"

Of course, among the strategies for dealing with stress there are the philosophical or quasi-religious anti-stress views such as those of Professor Selye. There are also some antiquated methods, which are nonetheless very human: Transcendental Meditation, yoga, acupuncture and moxibustion and even various forms of knitting or crocheting. And there are always alcohol, tobacco and caffeine, even though they may be regarded as the root of various ills by standard medical practice. From the view of stress theory alone, if these substances are used in accordance with TPO, then even though the result may not be "useful" stress, they might still be said to be considered necessary evils or stimuli, at least as far as dealing with stress is concerned. Yet whether or not one could say that human beings are "medicine-loving animals", it is true that many people place all their hope on the acquisition of a medicine for nearly every problem. The most attractive feature is of course that it is handy, one can take the medicine by oneself as one needs it. Moreover, it is a simple fact of history that medicine both in the East and the West has carried out its mission of treating and curing human ills through the administration of medicine.

However, as the historian Arnold Toynbee has pointed out, the degeneration of modern civilization can be thought to have begun with the successes of synthetic chemistry. The so-called new medicines and drugs are of course an important link in this chain of discoveries. To be sure, there were some essays critical of this outlook but the representative speaker at this conference, Linus Pauling, took a position which was quite close to that of Toynbee. Pauling is an American biochemist who has pioneered a revolution in modern chemistry. Not only is he the only person since Madame Curie to have been awarded two Nobel prizes but if it were possible to receive three it is said that he is more likely to do it than anyone else. One of the central points of his "Orthomolecular Medicine" is the adminsitration of large doses of Vitamin C, i.e., megavitamins.

Orthomolecular Medicine and Vitamin C

"This is no mere display of eccentricity. Fundamentally it is possible to engender a new field of medicine by merely changing the proportions of substances around the human body.

"Take Vitamin C for example. The minimum required dosage for an adult as established by the World Health Organization is 45 mg., the minimum amount needed to prevent scurvy. As a price paid for evolutionary progress chimpanzees and human beings lost the capacity to synthesize Vitamin C in their bodies and must thus actively seek sources of large quantities of Vitamin C in the environment to supply their needs."

This is Pauling's point of departure and he connects this with
the taking of Vitamin E also. These two vitamins are substances
which cannot be manufactured inside the human body but must be
gotten from the outside and ingested. And, in fact, his questioning
whether we get sufficient amounts of these vitamins from our food
alone is a bold and concrete way of calling to task our diet and
calling for an examination of our modern lifestyle. This is what he
has termed *orthomolecular medicine.*

Even though a certain degree of "inflation" probably was
inevitable it is nonetheless a generally accepted historical fact that
the "transnational" ceremony of awarding the Nobel prize, which
came into being at the turn of the century, did set a standard of
evaluation and recognition for modern civilization, honoring the
knowledge or intellect that supports it and even, although this is
sometimes difficult to see, stimulating worldwide altruism.

No one who has some acquaintance with chemistry needs to be
told about Pauling who started out as a chemist and who was
responsible for a reorganization of modern chemistry through the
introduction of quantum theory. His investigations in organic
chemistry naturally inclined him to interest himself progressively
in high level biochemistry and then to the sphere of human
problems. The occasion for his second Nobel prize, the Peace
Prize, for the Soviet-American Nuclear Test Ban project, was a
manifestation of true humanitarianism which is as rare as it is
necessary.

All this I knew from things I had read about him, but when he
spoke from his seat or took his tall frame to the podium for an
address I must say that I was deeply impressed. In front of that
audience, which included not a few pedestrian students such as
myself, he spoke without wasting a word about what he had named
orthomolecular medicine, which arose out of the beliefs and hypotheses he had gleaned from his work in the development of biochemistry. When he spoke one was impressed by two things. Here was
the figure of an old warrior who had fought innumerable intellectual

battles successfully and, although achieving victory, would still not rest and sheath his sword. But even more than this, one's feelings were enveloped in a way transcending ordinary perception by an inexhaustible love for all mankind, a love so vibrant that it sounds trivial to refer to it even as an ultimate altruism which gushes out, transcending life and death.

It is a fact however that the world's doctors, beginning with the American Medical Association, were not overly sympathetic to a Ph.D. in a nonmedical field intruding on physiology and medicine. He discussed many things, but the core of his hypothesis concerned Vitamin C in the human body. I'll pass over much of the long and complicated history of Vitamin C, but there are two important facts about this which should be noted. First, Vitamin C was discovered by Dr. Albert Szent-Gyorgyi in the center of stress physiology, the adrenal glands; and second, the eyeball is, in a sense, "pickled in vitamin C". In terms of the theory of stress both of these can be viewed as typical adaptive organs of the human body. Dr. Pauling's bold hypothesis that, "Highly evolved species such as humans and chimpanzees sacrificed the ability to synthesize Vitamin C in their bodies (dogs and other animals can perform this feat) and evolved by adapting," is at the present time a hypothesis which is difficult to account for since we don't know why this should have been the case.

However, even though it is available almost everywhere, or perhaps possibly because of that, Vitamin C has been paid little attention. Pauling's interest in and re-evaluation of Vitamin C most likely originated in a humanitarian feeling which would not let him tolerate that state of affairs, and his work contains powerful suggestions which transcend questions of his lack of experience in this specialty (questions of "proper" boundaries between academic disciplines).

Diet is most important to health and life

Modern stress constantly provides one with an awareness of one's environment in the changes occurring in human life, including communication and transportation. Even if clinical medicine is as yet far from attaining the "deep level psychological affirmations" in the organism which responds to stress, it is the case that the "social psychology" for the situation which supplies stress has already been incorporated in the field of clinical medicine.

However, this is an image of human beings dressed up by modern civilization, while the life of an individual naked human being, past or present, is actually centered on questions of food, clothing and shelter. (It is the full image or ideal type of human being which includes problems of sexuality also.)

Moreover, apart from the individual observations mentioned at the beginning of the chapter there is a broad, long-term health survey which covered thirty years in Japan and was developed in meticulous detail. According to a survey of approximately 700 villages and hamlets throughout the country, the condition which has the most profound relationship to long life is diet. For example, Shizuoka Province has a longevity rate of 3% but a neighboring village of Sumiyoshi in southern Izu has only a 2% rate. Since climatic conditions are identical the only thing which would account for the difference would seem to be the excessive intake of white rice and the insufficiency of vegetable intake in the diet of the people of Sumiyoshi. Moreover, the rapid increase in the longevity rate in Akita province which had been one of the most prominent short-lived areas in the country is conjectured to be due chiefly to a change in food, i.e., a decrease in intake of salt and white rice with an increase of vegetable products.

This sort of phenomenon, the relation of diet and longevity, seems to be applicable on a wider scale to a map of the long-lived regions of the world. It also seems to be congruent with the picture given by a map showing populations in terms of their degree of health.

The area of the world which has received the most attention for its reputation for longevity and health is the Caucasus area in and near the Soviet Union. This is an area which is not blessed with the best of climatic conditions or the ready means to support life; it is a harsh area. For that reason it is an illustration of the law of survival of the fittest, an example of the alloy of heredity and environment which Pavlov regarded as the fundamental condition of health and long life.

Further there is the fact that since the institution of the old age pension system in 1945 the number of people living to eighty-five and beyond has increased five-fold. One might infer from this that a decisive element of longevity is security in the foundations of one's life, i.e., the amelioration of basic stress conditions.

However, in most cases the physical and social environmental conditions are beyond the control, sometimes even in a most minor way, of the individual or the clinical physician. What is directly controllable, what can be modified in the daily life of these people to make them healthier and more resilient is their food, their diet.

In a word, lactic acid products (yogurt, etc.), protein, of course, and large amounts of vegetables and fruit on their dinner tables are their answer. They eat large quantities of *simple* food in the original sense of the word, i.e., food that has been tampered with or processed but very little.

The proliferation of mass-processed food reduces vitamins

Returning to the Pauling thesis, speaking only about Vitamin C now, to work on or cook the food is to destroy the Vitamin C. Nutrition specialists say that even in simply washing the food one-half the Vitamin C is lost. Even if there are foods like the varieties of potato which are tolerant of the heat in cooking (boiling, baking) and which have a protective covering or a "pre-body" for the C they contain, there is no telling how much damage is done to food's basic function of nourishing the body and its physiology by cooking and complicated preparation.

The same problem manifests itself in some fashion in all the varieties of food and food products as well as in their selection. Starting with the use of fire the human diet was greatly changed, i.e., cooked food became the norm.

The next major change was cultivation, agriculture and live-stock farming, and now an age of agribusiness, mass production and industrialization of food products.

There are a large number of reports dealing individually with these changes and the different products which result from them. But Dr. Pauling's suggestions are an exception since there are very few works which deal in a comprehensive way with the changes in food products. The reason is that this history is long and complex precisely because it is so intimately tied up with the life of every individual.

If one were to try to find another example of such a compre-hensive view one might cite the historian Arnold Toynbee's pro-nouncement referred to earlier that "the degeneration of human civilization began with the synthetic chemistry of the 19th cen-tury." Taken from the viewpoint of a clinical physician this judgement is quite easy to understand, for if one applies it to the content of one's daily diet, one finds an insufficiency of vitamins C and E as well as both yellow and green vegetables.

No matter how close a friend or acquaintance a patient may be it is impossible for a physician to sit across from him or her and monitor all their meals every day. Yet if one really wants to, it is possible to get some reports from them about their diet as part of the treatment program. Even from these incomplete reports it is clear that what the individual households have in common, at least as far as urban dwellers are concerned, is that their food has somehow become standardized. They have become the consumers of mass-produced foodstuff so that there is almost no difference among the individuals in their consumption patterns.

Avoiding the difficult and opting for the simple is an inescap-able feature of the mass production method, and it is quite understandable that, from the seller's point of view, buyers' pref-erences are more important than quality so that flavor is the primary concern for food products. Yet is this really the way things ought to be? Can we afford to let these matters stand in this way?

A modern health strategy begins with improving diet

One point that was enthusiastically and unanimously agreed to by the participants in this international stress conference was that there is an inseparable connection between the problems of stress and health, treatment and prevention of disease, as well as treatment of the aged and promotion of healthy longevity.

Unfortunately the conference was ultimately only able to touch on the edges of a strategy for dealing with stress. The general conclusion was, "It is precisely through enduring some measure of difficulties and lacks or some appropriate stress or U-stress (useful stress) that mental and physical resistance is strengthened and the door to health and longevity is opened." Which is to say that the research in various theories of nurturing the strength of the body's reactive capacity had just begun.

There is stress which can be submitted to and stress that can be avoided, but there is also stress which cannot be avoided, which is followed by shock and which develops into something fatal. Modern civilization and the modern urban lifestyle which intensifies this provide the "condensed milk of stress", and one need only reflect on the number of people who can freely change jobs or place of residence to make this clear.

Emergencies become commonplace and, ultimately, the only thing one can do about this state of affairs is to nourish and protect one's body. What everyone can do in this respect is to re-evaluate the food they eat, not merely in a purely negative fashion by avoiding contaminated foodstuff but by rectifying deficiencies in the present state through better selection and consumption.

As a reminder one need only keep in mind this simple but decisive summary: "Somehow, methods of cooking and the food market changed and now they cause a deficiency of vitamins C and E as well as the vegetable protein which would be gotten from green and yellow vegetables."

Modern medicine also is beginning to change from a discipline which began with the observation and treatment of individual illnesses to a discipline concerned with long-range health and the protection of an individual's life as a whole.

It seems as though the Soviet Bloc has pioneered this change in outlook and Japan, being at least nominally in the western bloc, has been slow to reflect this changing conception. However, in medicine what seems slow is often fast and there has been an unexpectedly rapid and realistic change in attitude beginning to manifest itself in Japan. The as yet unfamiliar phrase *orthomolecular medicine* may be thought of as the advance guard of this revolution.

Another element of this change is the reminder which I mentioned earlier. Much of what was thought to be common sense in nutrition studies up to now has been overthrown (the high-calorie theory is an extreme example). But it is a hard fact that "chronic starvation" of certain vitamins and proteins has promoted aging, and that a reduction in their storage and absorption after middle age is one cause of the "premature" outbreak of old age diseases. What are referred to here as "old age" diseases are all stress-related diseases such as reactive high blood pressure, heart disease, various types of digestive tract ulcers, some forms of cancer, diabetes, rheumatism, cataracts, many liver and kidney ailments, etc. In other words, it refers to almost all the internally caused diseases or what are usually called "adult diseases".

One can say perhaps that this sort of view is what one might expect of a medical outlook from a country based on a materialistic view since the answer is given in terms of the food consumed, but it is impossible to deny that it does shed light on a fundamental issue common to all mankind, i.e., the maintaining of health which is a crucial aspect of every individual's existence.

Re-evaluation of the past where food was medicine

The popularity of a phrase like "re-evaluate the old (past)" is one indicator of a turning point in civilization. Whatever comes of it, the interest in the acupuncture of ancient China suggests some changes occurring in the world's medical technology and outlook.

The emergence of Spirulina, which itself is also both old and new, is another instance of this. It lies between the categories of medicine and food. What was lost through the differentiations imposed by civilization is now being restored, rediscovered.

Even if the full implications are not yet available to the medical world, Spirulina, like the re-evaluation of the theory of stress, represents a new realm of research to which both society and medicine are turning their attention.

Chapter Thirteen

SPIRULINA—
THE MANNA OF THE FUTURE
Spirulina—a food resource for
an overpopulated world.

by Dr. Hiroshi Watarai, Ph.D., M.D.,
Director, Watarai Clinic, Tokyo

Spirulina—born in Africa, raised in Mexico

One evening after dinner while watching TV there were news reports of the butterbur flowers beginning to bud in Hokkaido, and in Tokyo's Akihnbarn (famed for its electronics and appliance outlets) the appliance dealers were bemoaning the lack of heating unit sales. Caught up by these stories we too began to talk about mild winters, with my wife remarking, "The winters in Mexico were warm too, weren't they?"

The two of us had joined a group tour for eight days beginning on December 30, 1977, to sunny Mexico. The tour was arranged by an airline and consisted of fifteen doctors, nine relatives and an escort.

I had a dream I wanted to realize through participation in this tour even though it was not on the schedule. This dream was to visit the caracol solar pond maintained by the Sosa Texcoco Company just outside Mexico City. It seems that "caracol" means "snail" in Spanish and the pond was called "caracol" because of its shape. But I did not come to Mexico all the way from Japan simply because I wanted to see a snail-shaped pond. In fact this caracol pond had become famous throughout the world for being the culturing ground for the algae, Spirulina, which had been attracting attention as "the food of the future for mankind". I wanted to check this out in person.

In May 1972, at the 2nd International Conference on Microbiological Protein held at M.I.T., Professor Clement of the French National Petroleum Research Institute reported, "a multi-cellular algae of the blue-green algae type which contains high quality protein has been found growing wild in Lake Chad in Africa. This deserves to be investigated as a possible important source of future protein." This report alone was enough to interest the various scholars and scientists in Spirulina throughout the world who were worried about the food supply problem.

With a world food crisis impending, interest in Algae grows

In Japan today there is almost no sense of urgency about a

food crisis, probably because there is a super abundance of rice. However, food specialists and nutritionists throughout the world have put great emphasis on the experimental development of microbiological protein in order to solve the problem of insufficient food supply caused by the planet's exploding population. One aspect of this is research into algae with high photosynthetic capacity. Up to now when one thought of green algae what came to mind was Chlorella and Scenedesmus, but with Professor Clement's report Spirulina came onto the stage as a third species commanding the attention of researchers. Because of this Professor Clement is likely to be regarded as the "mother of Spirulina", and with good reason, but even before her report there was a microbiologist who poured boundless energy and enthusiasm into research on this old-but-new species of algae. This man is Dr. Hiroshi Nakamura. It would be impossible to tell the story of Spirulina without including the work of Dr. Nakamura. Thus I shall ask Dr. Nakamura to relate the details of the history of research on Spirulina and shall confine myself to topics related more to my own experience.

There are some astounding things going on in the research on Spirulina in Japan today. Following in the footsteps of Dr. Nakamura there are reports by a large number of scholars such as Professor Hideo Ebine, Applied Microbiology Section Chief of the National Food Research Institute of the Ministry of Agriculture and Forestry and Professor Masayuki Katsumi of International Christian University, while on the medical front there is the fascinating research of people like Dr. Naoharu Fujii, a Tokyo internist and editor of the Japanese edition of this volume. According to these researchers Spirulina's most attractive properties are its abundance of nutritional elements, especially protein, its superior digestibility, and its fecundity. Since it is also relatively easy to harvest and dry, one can look forward to its mass production on a big industrial scale. Moreover, since it is a somewhat advanced life form there are not the sudden haphazard mutations which occur in bacteria and there is no danger of toxicity.

One more characteristic of this algae is its strong alkalinity, with its proper pH level being between 9 and 11. Because of this it is easy to prevent extraneous bacterial pollution and its absorption of carbon dioxide gas is good. Moreover, it can utilize carbonates (carbon salts) in place of carbon dioxide and, if afterwards there is a supply of strong energy from the sun, nothing more is required. It was this point that prompted Professor Clement, after extensive tests in various parts of France and Algeria, to select the caracol pond in sun-drenched Mexico. I arrived on one of the worst possible days, New Year's Eve, but through the kind offices of José Torello, the commercial manager for Sosa Texcoco, I was able to visit the caracol pond.

Growing Spirulina in strong sunlight

Even though it was New Year's Eve in the northern hemisphere the Mexican sun was strong and bright, and the people at the plant were kind enough to lend my wife a sun hat. This was probably why my wife later mentioned Mexico when we were talking about mild winters. I also took up my pen to write this long overdue article while giving myself up to the deep emotion I felt on seeing the Spirulina growing in the huge caracol pond. It is said that there are no fish in the pond and the building on the opposite shore is reflected on the surface of the water which displays a variety of colors from blue through blue-green to a dark green. Therein occurs the unending division and propagation of the Spirulina through the asexual reproduction characteristic of the blue-green algae. The countless bubbles which seemed to be dancing on the surface of the water were bubbles of carbon dioxide being expelled into the air. I was deeply impressed looking at this enormous world of photosynthesis so near at hand. I was informed that the mechanics of photosynthesis in blue-green algae were quite different from other algae and the advanced animal forms.

Blue-green algae developed on earth at the earliest stage of evolution over three billion years ago. The blue-green algae have no nucleus and the infracellular organs (organs internal to the cell) such as the chloroplast and mitochondria have not yet been differentiated and therefore it absorbs the sun's energy with the red pigment, blue pigment and chlorophyll-a which exist in its stratified membranes. The reason that land plants have a relatively low production rate for their size is their longevity, i.e., it requires years or decades to produce an organism. Thus even when Chlorella is cultivated in the open, the amount of protein obtained in a year would be thirty times that which could be gotten by using the same area of land to grow both soybeans and wheat in succession. It is then small wonder that Spirulina which contains 1.3 times as much protein as Chlorella should become the center of attention.

Presently the greatest use for the Spirulina imported into Japan from Mexico is for fish farming where it is used as high protein feed for eels, trout and fish which have red pigment such as shrimp, sea bream, colored carp, rainbow carp (koi) and goldfish. Apparently it is quite effective not only because of the protein but also because of the colorants it contributes such as chlorophyll, phycocyanin and xanthophyll.

What most deeply impressed me on the trip to Mexico was that a very large number of the foods crucial to the world at this time had their roots in plants cultivated on the "new continents" in places like Mexico. Among the cultivated plants developed by the new world agriculture there are many superior products such as corn and kidney beans as well as other varieties of bean, squash, tomato, cayenne pepper, black pepper, peanut, pineapple, potato and sweet potato. Corn, particularly, was the basic staple of ancient Mexican culture and even today is being used in 90% of the staple foods, taking such forms as tortillas, tamales and the like.

India developing large-scale production

Let us now turn to India. India has a population of 650 million people and is struggling to achieve self-sufficiency in food production. Spirulina is one of the means they are using to reach this goal. Part of this was reported by the Asahi Shimbun, a national newspaper, (May 24, 1979, evening edition) with a one-page illustrated article entitled "Indian Scientific Technology Strives for Self-Sufficiency" and in the section entitled "Food for the Future" the paper describes the state of Spirulina cultivation. I should like to quote a portion of that article here:

"India, which until quite recently did not produce enough food to provide the minimum required to sustain life for all her people, is now rapidly pursuing research into the production of 'the food of the future' to prepare for the future world food crisis. At the center of this research effort is the Central Food Technology Research Center in Mysore. Since 1973 a joint Indian-German algae project has been conducted here with two species of algae being the central focus. These are the blue-green algae, Spirulina, and the green algae, Scenedesmus, which is closely related to Chlorella. They use a low cost, large volume method of cultivation in an outdoor cultivation tank."

The article also contained a photograph with the caption, "The outdoor algae cultivation site which will hopefully be a source of protein for the future. India also is attempting to break through the food crisis with the help of Spirulina." I pray they are successful. In Japan too, the Greater Japan Ink and Chemicals Industries, Inc. (DIC) has completed a pure culture factory in Thailand to produce pure Spirulina for use as a new food for human consumption and has already gone into mass production. In these ways Spirulina has taken big steps in the direction of becoming a future source of high protein for mankind.

The cultivation of new plants is the basis of a new culture

When a specialist who has excellent knowledge of his field speaks, one sometimes finds oneself nodding assent or muttering, "Oh, I see," (even though what is said is quite novel). Sasuke Nakao, who is well known for his expertise in breeding, has a very interesting view on the nature of culture and I should like to outline that view as a way of concluding this essay.

When the word "culture" ("bunka" in Japanese) is used, one immediately thinks of art, literature, music, technology, etc., but not of farming or techniques of cultivation for these are commonly thought to be external to culture. But the Japanese "bunka" is in fact a translation of the English "culture" or the German "kultur" both of which originally refer to cultivating. It is from this cultivation that all the higher cultures were born. Thus farming is the root of culture and cultivating plants and raising vegetables is mankind's most important cultural asset. Thus it is in the process of evolving from wild growing plants to cultivating plants that one finds the concrete manifestations of human intelligence, industry and permanence, and one also finds in the evolution of seed cultures the permanent record of the intelligence and industry of the human race.

Nucleus

Spirulina, like all blue green algae, has a high percentage of chlorophyll as well as other pigments. These pigments are stored in the chloroplasts which contain layers or grana which are interconnected. An electron micrograph of an Anabaena blue green alga shows the lack of a clearly defined membrane around the nucleus. The structures to be seen as layers in the cytoplasm are the chloroplasts responsible for photosynthesis.

glycine + succinyl CoA

$\downarrow$ ALA-synthetase (pyridoxal phosphate)

$HOOC \cdot CH_2 \cdot CH_2 \cdot CO \cdot CH_2 NH_2$
δ-aminolevulinic acid (ALA)

$\downarrow$ +ALA

porphobilinogen (PBG)

$\downarrow$ +3PBG

uroporphyrinogen III

$\downarrow$

coproporphyrinogen III

$\downarrow$

protoporphyrin $\longrightarrow$ heme $\longleftrightarrow$ cytochromes

$\downarrow$ $\qquad$?

Mg protoporphyrin $\xrightarrow{\quad ? \quad}$ phycobilins

$\downarrow$

Mg protoporphyrin monomethyl ester

$\downarrow$ 3 steps

Mg divinyl pheoporphyrin a_5

$\downarrow$

Mg vinyl pheoporphyrin a_5 (Mg VP)
(protochlorophyllide)

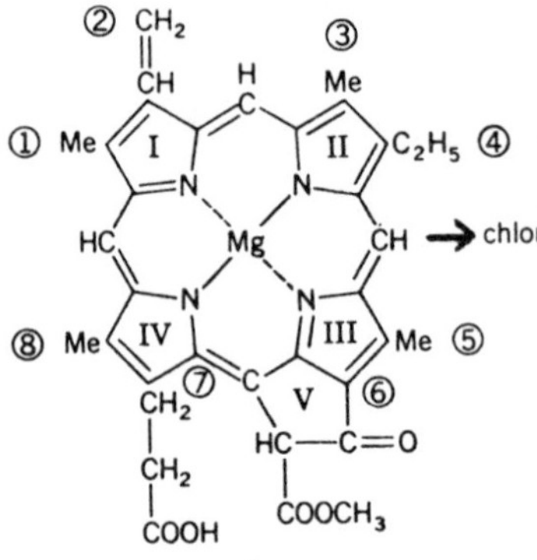

$\rightarrow$ chlorophyll c

$\downarrow$

Mg VP holochrome

$\downarrow$

chlorophyllide holochrome?

$\downarrow$

chlorophyll a $\longrightarrow$ chlorophyll b
$\qquad$ chlorophyll d
$\downarrow$? $\longrightarrow$ bacteriochlorophyll a
$\qquad$ bacteriochlorophyll "b"

(chlorophyll)$_n$

Structure of chlorophyll a

$(C_{55}H_{72}O_5N_4Mg)$.

Editor's Note:

The two major pigments of all proto
plasm, green chlorophyll and re
heme, are synthetized along th
same metabolic pathway which bio
synthesizes protoporphyrin. Startin
from the same building blocks c
glycine amino acid and succinic acic
they are converted by enzymes i
steps identical in plants and humans

The structure of Chlorophyll is base
on the porphyrin pyrrole ring, a re
pigment common in seaweeds, al
gae, chlorophyll and hematin whic
is the red pigment of blood and re
and green pigments of bile. The onl
difference is that chlorophyll ha
magnesium at its center and hemati
has iron at its center (see page 20;
for detailed explanation).

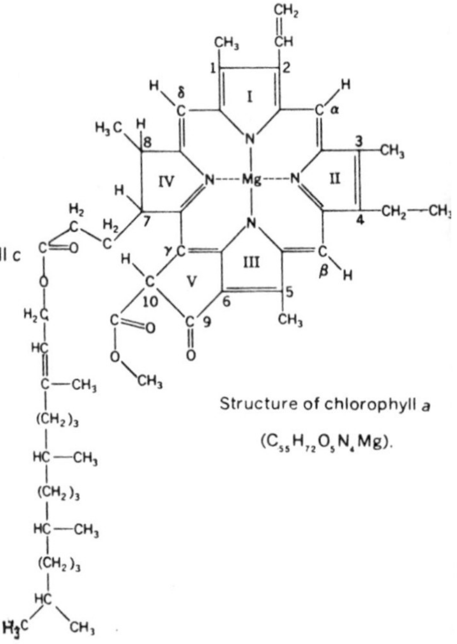

Chapter Fourteen

"GREEN BLOOD" OR CHLOROPHYLL'S POSITIVE EFFECTS ON THE ENTIRE BODY
The function of Chlorophyll which Spirulina contains in abundance.

by Makoto Uno, Science Writer

Chlorophyll is "green blood"

I thought that I would write about why chlorophyll is called "green blood," but before I do I should like to touch briefly on the nature of chlorophyll and chloroplasts.

Chloroplasts are widely contained in plant cells and are granules exceeded in size only by the nucleus. They, together with the mitochondria, are the important cellular organs in terms of energy exchange. Plastids (color bodies) are divided into three types according to the pigment they contain, so that one which contains chlorophyll is a chloroplast while those that contain carotin or some other red pigment are chromoplasts and those without color are leucoplasts. These have all developed through evolution from identical origins and thus have a very strong mutual interrelationship. The most important of the plastids is the chloroplast which is the seat of photosynthesis.

Chloroplasts are plastids which contain chlorophyll and are found in the cells of all the leaves as well as roots and stalks which have green color. In higher plants they are 2-3 microns in size and often take the shape of a lens or an ellipse. However, they assume a variety of shapes depending on the plant, e.g., in hoshimidoro they are star-shaped, in aomidoro they are spirals, and in Chlorella they are saucer-shaped. This distribution of chloroplasts in the tissue cells differs according to the position or state of the cells, e.g., in epidermal cells it is known that chloroplasts move towards the direction of light.* Seen through an optical telescope chloroplasts appear to be no more than green granules, but if one views them through an electron microscope they display a variety of detailed structures.

In short, the chloroplast has a substrate or supportive framework

---

*Editor's note: The well-known phenomenon of etiolosis, or stretching towards light by plants, may be also repeated in brain cells where we have the process of neurobiotoxis or the growing of axons and nerve cells towards areas of greater stimulation. To stimulate or excite a cell causes it to move towards or away from the source of stimulus if it is beneficial or harmful.

which is called the "stroma" and is light green in color along with a deep green granular portion called the "grana". The "grana" comes from a stratified column of double membraned discs piled one on the other. The number of discs which form a "grana" vary between two and fifty, with an undeveloped chloroplast having only few and a fully developed one having many. In the stroma a small granula can be seen which is thought to be a ribosome (the locus of the synthesis of protein). Moreover, microbiological research has made it clear that DNA (deoxyribonuclear acid, the carrier of genetic information) is also present here.

The chromoplasts are plastids which contain colorants (pigments) other than cholorophyll and are found in the cells of orange-colored bodies such as the root of a carrot, squash, or the yellow petals of the Japanese globe flower (Kenia-Jap. *yamabuki*)

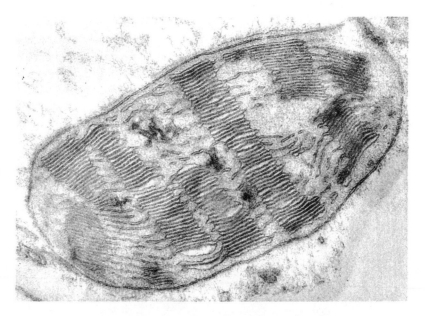

The grana of a chloroplast from a tobacco leaf multiplied 30,000 times shows alternate layers of protein as well as the membrane surrounding the chloroplast which separates it from the cytoplasm of the cell. Inside the chloroplast of a blue green alga the grana is made up of tiny thylakoid sacs which contain the phycobilin and carotenoid pigments.

and cayenne peppers. Chiefly the chromoplasts include the carotenoids.*

Leucoplasts are colorless plastids (color pigment bodies) which
are found in the seeds of higher plants, in the subterranean cells in
the white portions of striped or speckled leaves, etc. They are
classified according to the material they store. Thus those that
contain starch are termed amyloplasts, those with fats are called
lipoplasts, those with protein are called protein plasts (proteide
plasts, albumenoplasts etc.). If a seed is made to sprout in a dark
place, chlorophyll is not formed and the plastids remain leucoplasts,
but if this sprout is brought into the light they are converted into
chloroplasts. Consider the skin of a cayenne pepper which is
green-colored chloroplasts in the beginning but which change to
chromoplasts as the skin turns red or even the carrot in which the
leucoplasts turn into yellow/red chromoplasts. There are indeed a
a wide variety of transitions. Yet there are some restrictions on
permissible transitions. You can have a leucoplast change into a
chloroplast and then into a chromoplast and you can have a
leucoplast directly change into a chromoplast, but you cannot have
a chromoplast in which all the chlorophyll is gone change back
into a chloroplast.**

This, then, is a short outline of the relation between chloroplasts and chlorophyll. Now let us go on to discuss the relation
between chlorophyll and the hemoglobin contained in the red blood
cells (erythrocytes).

---

*Editor's Note: An important red pigment of Spirulina is Porphyrin, consisting of
pyrrole rings which are the active nucleus of chlorophyll cells and hemoglobin and
other cytochromes. When porphyrin pigments dominate the green they mix red and
green together making the Spirulina black or dark brown. Light brings out the greens
and blues and decays the red.

**Editor's Note: These rules are scientific orthodoxy but in Dr. Hills' collection of
Spirulina cultures we have had white leucoplasts in Spirulina change within 24 hours
into chloroplasts, chromoplasts and back into chloroplasts by forming new cells
while the old cells die off, become brown or go dormant. The key seems to be
nitrogen starvation or its opposite.

Similarity of chlorophyll and hemoglobin
in molecular structure

If one were to ask, "Why is human blood red?" the answer
would be, "Because of the red pigment of the hemoglobin contained in the red blood cells." Similarly, the green color of the
foliage of a plant is due to the green color of the chlorophyll in the
cells of the leaves. The hemoglobin in the blood is a combination
of a special protein called "globin" and a colorant called "heme".
The red blood cells, filled with hemoglobin, float along in the blood
serum and travel through the animal's entire body. The chlorophyll
in plants also combines with protein to form chloroplasts but,
unlike the red blood cells, the chloroplasts are restricted to a small
portion of the cells and do not travel about the interior of the plant.

Well then why is chlorophyll called 'green blood'?

Chlorophyll is a chemical substance formed from a variety of
different atoms but its fundamental chemical structure is a ring
formed by a grouping of four so-called pyrrole rings. Chlorophyll is
nearly always thought of only in connection with the foliage of
plants and it seems like a very specific, almost unique, chemical
substance, but in fact there are many substances in the natural
world which have the same sort of chemical structure. These are
all grouped together under the name "porphyrin pigments". Thus
chlorophyll is one of the porphyrin pigments as is the pigment of
the hemoglobin in blood serum. The pigments of catalase (an
enzyme which breaks down hydrogen peroxide) found in both
animals and plants as well as peroxidase (similar to catalase but it
is an enzyme which does not act on hydrogen peroxide when there
is no oxidizable substance present) are also porphyrin pigments.
Both chlorophyll and hemoglobin are somewhat complicated substances, each being a ring formed by four pyrrole rings. These
complicated substances did not just suddenly appear in nature but
came into being as a result of a long process of evolution.

First the pentagonal-shaped pyrrole rings were formed from the
basic elements, i.e., carbon, hydrogen, oxygen, nitrogen, etc. Then
four of these came together to form the ring-shaped structure called

the porphyrin ring. Then a number of chemical substances attached themselves to the circumference of that complex ring and the various porphyrin pigments came into being. Since both chlorophyll and hemoglobin pigment both passed through this same course of development, there must be somewhere in the bodies of living things a precursor substance which makes the rings, i.e., some chemical substance which underlies the ring formation. This reasoning is correct. For example, there is a root nodule pigment of reddish hue (gingery hue) in the root nodules of plants, and in animals the respiration pigment, chlorochlurine of invertebrates corresponds to this. For this reason there are a number of similarities between chlorophyll and hemoglobin pigment. In the case of chlorophyll, magnesium is at the center of the porphyrin, it exhibits a green color, and is connected with synthesizing activity. In the case of hemoglobin, iron is at the center of the porphyrin, it exhibits a red color, and is connected with the activity of analysis or decomposition. Although there is the same porphyrin pigment in both cases, the chlorophyll has magnesium, is green and is engaged in synthesis of material, i.e., photosynthesis, while the hemoglobin pigment has iron, is red and is engaged in the breaking down of material or respiration. These analogies are indeed very interesting (and thought-provoking).

Moreover, since these two pigments have almost identical basic forms, chlorophyll can be transformed into the hemoglobin pigment. That is to say that when we eat chlorophyll and the magnesium which was at its center is extracted, iron comes in to fill the vacancy and the chlorophyll molecule changes to hemoglobin. The supposition that this would mean an increase in the quantity of blood is not at all outlandish. In fact, there is animal experiment data which show that when the animals were fed slightly broken down chlorophyll molecules the red blood cell count increased.

Chlorophyll heightens liver functions and promotes regeneration (metastasis)

Let us now briefly discuss the function of chlorophyll in terms of medical therapy.

In the 1920s and 30s great strides were made in the basic medical and chemical aspects of chlorophyll research. After 1940 America became the center of research on chlorophyll especially with an extensive reexamination of its value for pharmacological applications as a medicine. In any case, the virtues of chlorophyll attracted much attention because of the dramatic effect it had on general wounds and purulent infections. How, then, does the chlorophyll function? First it has been shown that chlorophyll has the effect of heightening the efficiency of all the tissues and organs in the body. To give an example, in experiments conducted on muscles and nerves it was found that chlorophyll aided the transmission of stimuli and that muscles and nerves which did not function because of exhaustion were restored to an operative state with the administration of chlorophyll.

It also has effects on the heart, i.e., the contractions are stronger and the diastolic period longer. In other words since the time for transmission of stimuli from the atrium of the heart to the ventricles is slow, the heart beat slows down, and with the strength of contraction high, the function of the heart as a whole is made more efficient. Since the expansion of the peripheral blood vessels (capillaries) is even more marked than the strengthening of the heart's function, there is a tendency for the blood pressure to decrease. Further, it is notable that if one administers a solution of 1/2000th chlorophyll for a heart which has lost its activity through poison or exhaustion the functions are revived.

Chlorophyll is said to be good for constipation and this is because it encourages the peristaltic action of the intestines. The respiration rate and volume are also increased and thus it counteracts the respiratory paralysis caused by drugs like morphine. With respect to the uterus it increases the tension and strengthens the contractive power of the uterine muscles, which is very desirable at the time of the delivery of a baby. Chlorophyll is said to accelerate metastasis in general but in any case it seems that nitrogen metabolism becomes quite lively. This means that the basic metabolism is heightened. Since it also has a stimulative effect on the blood-producing organs similar to that of iron, it has a rather clearly marked blood-producing activity. The fact that chlorophyll has a connection with blood production apart from the close similarity of chemical structure between it and hemoglobin pigment is of great interest for scientists and physicians.

Chlorophyll prevents wound infection

Many clinical physicians have become excited by the basic data that has been gathered on chlorophyll's beneficial pharmaceutical properties. At first, about forty years ago, chlorophyll was tried in the treatment of wounds because of its ability to enliven tissue functions and as tissue culture experiments continued they confirmed that the chlorophyll does indeed make tissue activity more energetic. But since at that time they did not yet have the technology requisite to separate chlorophyll from the plant pigments they surmised that the substance which was effective as a disinfectant was not chlorophyll but carotine (this pigment exists in the green leaves along with chlorophyll and in the body of an animal it is broken up to become Vitamin A). Subsequently, however, it was discovered that the magnesium which is contained in chlorophyll plays an important role in wound healing. What sorts of things happen when chlorophyll is used in the treatment of wounds?

For example, when anaerobic bacteria (bacteria which grow where there is no oxygen and die if exposed to air, such as soil bacteria and tetanus bacteria) invade an open wound they give rise to a powerful and noxious odor which is dispelled by chlorophyll. Chlorophyll also has a sterilizing capacity and acts to prevent the growth of bacteria. This prevents infection of the wound and encourages the formation of new granulation as well. Thus the chlorophyll has a doubly beneficial effect.

In addition it is known that chlorophyll is a desiccant, drying wounds and limiting secretions. What is most encouraging is that it has no side effects. In any case, by using chlorophyll the amount of antibiotics that must be used can be cut by 50% or more.

Effective for ulcers and digestive inflammation

Many Japanese suffer from problems with their digestive system and it is thus particularly welcome to hear that chlorophyll is good for this sort of problem. For example, it is said that chlorophyll is good for diseases such as ulcers, excessive stomach acid, chronic gastritis, and gastric atonic condition (lack of strength in stomach). In the case of excess stomach acid, for example, chlorophyll helps to regulate the acidity of the gastric juices, i.e., when one takes chlorophyll the stomach's acidity is normalized. Further, if one does a gastric-juice-occult-blood test in the case of ulcers and then continues to administer chlorophyll internally the occult blood reaction disappears. Subjective symptoms such as stomach pain and nausea which are often associated with these illnesses are alleviated relatively rapidly with the taking of chlorophyll internally.

The hypothesis that chlorophyll might be effective against ulcers of the digestive system seems to have resulted from the observation that skin ulcers and wounds healed faster when chlorophyll was applied to them. Now it is clear not only that chlorophyll is effective against gastric and duodenal ulcers but that it also helps to prevent the occurrence of ulcers.

Now when one asks why chlorophyll should prevent ulceration the best hypothesis seems to be that the chlorophyll acts on pepsin and checks the digestive action of the pepsin (an enzyme which breaks down protein). (Gastric juice and pepsin, together with the cooperation of acids, especially hydrochloric acid, breaks down protein into protease and peptone). Indeed experiments have shown that chlorophyll does indeed check the digestive activity.* Moreover, chlorophyll is anti-allergenic and this is effective in the case of allergic gastritis, gastric ulcers resulting from allergies as well as other allergic diseases. Chlorophyll's effectiveness thus has come to be recognized in fields from surgery, dermatology and gynecology to

---

Editor's note: This may explain the well known effect of Spirulina on appetite with people who are fasting. Weight watchers and dieting people have all reported they never feel hungry when taking Spirulina.

ophthalmology, nose and throat fields and dentistry.

Is chlorophyll's semiconductive activity
the source of a mysterious power?

In recent years it has been pointed out that chlorophyll has the character of a semiconductor and this gave rise to much discussion in the field. When normal metals are heated their electrical resistance increases so that it becomes difficult for electrical current to pass through them but a semiconductor acts in precisely the opposite way, i.e., when the temperature is raised it conducts (but does so very little if at all when the temperature is low). The semiconductors that are best known are germanium, silicon, selenium, etc.

Semiconductors can also be transformed from insulators to good conductors through the action of light, electromagnetism, radiation and the like as well as heat rays. This is due to the energy of the light, infrared rays or whatever causes free electrons to jump to the conduction zone in the semiconductor and thus the electricity flows. The conducting of electricity indicates that free electrons are present and when a metal which has free electrons is struck by light, electrons escape from the surface of the metal (photoelectric effect). Thus when a semiconductor is heated or struck by light an electric current flows which is to say that a semiconductor has the ability to change light energy or thermal energy into electricity.

Recently Professor Calvin (a Nobel prize winner) and his group at the University of California found that free electrons are generated when light strikes a chloroplast. The basis for this apparently was that where there are free electrons present a portion of the high frequency light waves are absorbed. Ultimately the fact that free electrons are generated when light strikes chlorophyll is a straightforward demonstration that it has the character of a semiconductor. Thereupon Professor Calvin and his team exposed chlorophyll to sunlight and one of the chlorophyll's electrons was sent flying. The electrons became a conductor moving spontaneously from chlorophyll to chlorophyll to gather together in one place. By going through this process the chlorophyll changes light energy to electrical energy when struck by light.

This electrical energy finally takes the carbon from the carbon dioxide in the atmosphere and synthesizes carbon compounds. When the electron (H_1) escapes from the chlorophyll the vacancy it creates is filled by an electron from water and this means that the water molecule (H_2O) is broken up into a molecule of hydrogen and an oxygen atom (H_1O). It was from experiments such as this that it was determined that the chlorophyll makes use of the light's energy and how it happens.

When one takes chlorophyll and exposes that green liquid to ultraviolet radiation the chlorophyll shines red. This is because it absorbs part of the ultraviolet radiation's energy and emits the longer wavelength red light. This sort of light is called fluorescence. Because the red light emitted by the chlorophyll has wavelengths of 6750 and 7300 angstroms (1 angstrom = one one-hundred-millionth of a centimeter: $1/10^8$ cm) it generally coincides with the peak of red light in chlorophyll's absorption spectrum curve. However, even if one exposes plant leaves in which there is photosynthetic activity to ultraviolet radiation this sort of fluorescence is not produced. This is because the light's energy is used up in the process of photosynthesis. But when the chlorophyll alone is taken from the leaf, then since the energy which would have been used in photosynthesis is not used to synthesize carbon compounds and so becomes fluorescence and is emitted into the atmosphere. So goes the explanation.

Even though chlorophyll absorbs energy, if there is no mechanism for it to drive that energy into photosynthesis the chlorophyll eventually breaks down or dissipates. Thus chlorophyll captures the energy of light and converts it to electrical energy and it seems that this ability of chlorophyll to act as a semiconductor will soon have important pharmacological implications.

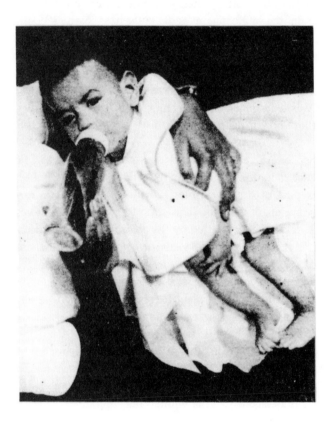

In Mexico the government institutes and universities have done studies on the addition of 10% Spirulina to babies' milk and also on the malnutrition of young children. These studies resulted in government approval of Spirulina as a new food.

Chapter Fifteen

SPIRULINA IS A GENUINE HEALTH FOOD
Securing health safety and efficacy in an age of un-"health foods", proved by several scientists.

by Kasaku Takashima, Medical Journalist

Just what is a "health food"?

"It seems that Greater Japan Ink and Chemicals Industrial
Company has started to work on an anti-cancer medication." It was
about three of four years ago that someone gave me this bit of
"information". Greater Japan Ink and Chemicals Industrial Co.—
DIC (Dainihon Inki Kagaku) is a comprehensive chemicals manu-
facturer with a strong interest in ink as well as resins, synthetics,
plastics, etc. The Kawamura Institute for Physical and Chemical
Research which presently acts as the central research organ for
Greater Japan Ink and Chemicals was preceeded by the Nitto
Institute for Physical and Chemical Research. Greater Japan Ink
inherited this as it were and moved it into the field of biochemistry.
It has already produced several feed and pharmaceutical products.

This being the case it was not strange that the company would
embark on the development of an anti-cancer medication. Yet after
this report on the project no further information was forthcoming;
the reports just stopped. Just after this, however, I heard a new
report that Greater Japan Ink and Chemicals was about to market
a health food product called "Spirulina". This was last summer. It
seems that the rumor about the anti-cancer medication was a
garbled version of the company's work on Spirulina.

But just what is Spirulina? Not only is the word hard for
Japanese to pronounce but it is not the sort of word that one would
remember after hearing it once. God knows what language the
word came from! This is the sort of thing that ran through my mind
at the time. It was not until later that I discovered that the word
was derived from the Latin and meant "a spiral or helix".

Speaking of linguistic investigations I have been bothered by a
phrase which became popular in Japan about five years ago—the
phrase "health food product." What is the definition of a "health
food product"? No matter whom I've asked, no one seemed to
know, and so one time I asked Professor Yuichiro Goto of Keio
University's Medical School. Professor Goto was quite indignant,
saying: "If there really is some difference in the health of those
people who use such food products regularly for a fixed period of

time and those who do not, then those food products could be
properly called health food products. But most of the so-called
health food products available today have no such experimental
validation. The problem is really the fact that the Ministry of
Health and Welfare should allow the unrestricted use of such an
ambiguous designation."

When I enquired at the Ministry of Health and Welfare about
this I found that the Ministry did not use that phrase at all. "Of
course we're not the sponsors of such a phrase; perhaps it might be
best to check with the Ministry of Agriculture and Forestry."
When I did so I received the same negative reply, together with the
suggestion that I ask Hiroyuki Iwao, Chief of the Applied Foods
Section of the National Institute of Nutrition who might have an
idea of the origin of the phrase. Unfortunately the Institute did not
possess any hard data on the subject either but they did give me a
hint by saying that the appearance of so-called "Hauser Food
Products" might have been the precursor of the current fad for
"health food products" in Japan.

The "health food product" craze
resulted from distrust of drugs

This was the first time I had even heard of "Hauser Food
Products" much less having tried them, but I thought that this
reference might be a lead so I began assembling material. In the
journal of social thought, *History of Social Conditions in the
Showa Period* (1926-Present) (Showa Sesoshi) which was published from 1945-70, there appeared the following leader and
article on the page for May 1954 by Iwasaki and Kato:

"The Hauser Method of Rejuvenation in Vogue: Mixers Sell Well"

Gaylord Hauser's *How to Live Long and Stay Young*, which
was a best seller in America has been introduced to Japan with
dramatic results. In Tokyo's Nihonbashi and Shinjuku 'Hauser
Gymnasiums' have been constructed and there is now a restaurant
on the Ginza which features 'Hauser Cooking.'

"The idea is that 'you will be healthy and vigorous from the next day' if you drink a mixture of the 5 astounding foods', i.e. fresh fruit and vegetable juice, wheat germ, molasses, etc. Supposedly it has all sorts of virtues and benefits such as making one thinner, lowering one's blood pressure and even making one smarter. This has made it quite popular, as one might expect.

"Because of the requirement of making fresh vegetable juice for this method the sales of mixers have increased dramatically. Many office workers have bought these 14,000-15,000 mixers ($41-43 at the exchange rate of the time), even when they had to resort to the monthly payment plan."

Seven years later on December 25, 1961 the Asahi Shimbun (Newspaper) reflected on trends of the year in an article entitled "The Health Boom" as follows:

"When one thinks about it this might have been termed 'the year of the health boom.' In April or so there was a great general enthusiasm for fresh juice and then along came the apples and honey contingent. Even department stores set up 'Health Corners' or 'Health and Vigor Counters' to sell health foods exclusively. 'Hauser foods' which had enjoyed a boom some years ago were brought out of the backrooms and prominently displayed in store windows.

"If one inspected the display cases one found calcium to prevent acidification of the blood, striped bamboo powder, mineral water, health kelp, health tea, etc. Naturally there were all sorts of vitamins and nutritional supplements in pill or capsule form being sold as usual and there was a great popularity of famous doctors revealing their health methods in magazines and newspapers. It was as though health control had become a national cause at election time."

Looking at this article in the Asahi it seems that we can reasonably date the health boom in Japan as having begun in 1960 or 61. The article uses the term "health food" (kenko shoku) but the term "health food product" (kenko shokuhin does not appear to have come into currency until later.

It is now twenty years later. What is most important now, in my estimation, is not the origin of the term "health food product" but its meaning. In essence the things which are now classified as health food products were at one time sold in limited geographic areas by merchants who dealt with steady customers. For that reason each of the products has its own special local flavor and style. But at some point the times changed and we entered an age of a "health boom", partly due to a dissatisfaction with medicines on the part of the general public. It's almost a cliché to say that the Japanese are fond of medicines but what put a damper on this was the general inspection of over 40,000 medicinal items which started in 1971. A full-scale check on the effectiveness of medicines had begun. The first report on the results was published at the end of February 1973. There were over 800 instances where the claims for medicinal effectiveness were simply lies or deliberate deception and these were exposed to public view. There were also many medicines which were decertified (prohibited for sale) when their pharmaceutical effectiveness was shown to be false.

With this investigation we passed into an age of distrust of medicines, but at the same time people began to re-evaluate and look with favor on traditional herb remedies as well as food products which had the title of natural food products or health food products. Basically the immediate cause or occasion for this investigation was the thalidomide disaster. The fact that side effects from a medicine taken as a sleeping aid could cause the birth of phocomelic deformed babies ('seal-limb' babies) taught people the danger of medicine.

It has been said since ancient time that there is only a hair's breadth between medicines and poisons and this incident brought the truth of this saying home to the entire country. Naturally this would cause any person to become apprehensive about synthetic medicines and feel attracted to health foods or natural foods.

Dangerous food products abound!

In this fashion Japan's pharmaceutical establishment lost its customers to health foods as a result of an investigation for which it was itself ultimately responsible, but in the health food industry which benefited from this investigation there began to emerge opportunists who thought they could make a killing out of this distrust of medicine.

In July 1978 the National Welfare Center, an extra-departmental body of the Economic Planning Agency which is responsible for dealing with consumer complaints about products, issued a pamphlet entitled "Health Food Products—Exploring the Problems". According to this report most of those having complaints were women of middle age or older. This is the group which has the most anxiety about health problems for themselves or their husbands. The following is a typical complaint related in the pamphlet.

Ms. A. (70) of Yamanashi Province had suffered from rheumatism for many years. Her extremities (hands and feet) were so stiff that she couldn't even hold her chopsticks. In the waiting room of a clinic one day she heard of a health food by the name of Kansai which supposedly was effective for rheumatism and so she immediately went out and bought some. It was sold in pill form, costing 4500 yen for 80 tablets. On the label was the following statement: "This is an alkaline food product made from natural plant leaves, roots, and pollen formed into pills with honey and the like."

When Ms. A. took these pills, the stiffness and pain quickly stopped and it seemed as though she had been cured as if by magic. The effects were, to say the least, dramatic. Her physician was quite surprised at this rapid cure and in fact was a bit worried because the food seemed almost too effective. He then asked Dr. Hiroshi Migushima, a Tokyo University physiotherapist and internist, to analyze this food, Kansai. The results showed the presence of adrenocortical hormones. These are not found naturally in the leaves of plants and the like but were chemically added.

Adrenocortical hormones are hormones secreted by the adrenal gland. They were first successfully extracted in crystal form in 1948 by the American biochemist, Kelden. When Dr. Hench, a rheumatism specialist at the Mayo Clinic, administered this hormone to patients remarkable results were obtained. Patients who were afflicted so severely that they could not walk and were confined to bed got out of bed and began walking. The work of these two scientists was subsequently recognized by the awarding of Nobel prizes.

This hormone has also been used in Japan since 1952 or 53 for a wide spectrum of diseases including rheumatism, collagen disease, digestive tract diseases and the like, so its effectiveness is well known. But because it has rather serious side effects it is not allowed to be used without the supervision of a doctor. Using this tends to give one a "moon face", i.e., rounding of the facial outline and after prolonged constant use the bones become fragile and break easily under the slightest provocation. This product which was sold as a "health food product" in fact contained a restricted and extremely dangerous ingredient. According to a study by the National Police Agency violations of this kind of the Drugs, Cosmetics and Medical Instruments Act are relatively common, i.e., over 400 occur per annum. The National Police takes the following stand on this question:

"In the background of this sort of incident there are a number of factors. One is an increased desire to promote health which accompanies the rise in the people's standard of living, while another is the anxiety with respect to serious or incurable diseases. It cannot be denied that there is also a distrust of existing medication because of the possibility of damage resulting from their use.

"These 'health food products' are presently enjoying a boom but there are no legal controls on their standards of manufacture or method of distribution.

"Judging from those that have been arrested it seems that they have a cavalier attitude towards the law and feel that they should make as much as they possibly can in a short period and then even if they have to pay a small fine they are still way ahead of the game. There are indeed cases where such violators were let off with a fine even though they had illicitly made millions of dollars.

"In order to combat this it is necessary for the consumers themselves to become more wary of and resistant to both medicines and health foods."

As the National Police point out it is indeed a grave problem that there are no legal controls on manufacturing standards for health foods. In the case of medicines there are a number of checks and double checks of its safety and if the safety of the medication is not verified it is not licensed to be sold.

Even Chlorella gave rise to side effects

Thus there is no mechanism for checking out food products; they are left completely alone. I myself did a bit of investigation into Spirulina on just this point. The reason for this was that when one speaks of Spirulina most people will at some point invite or make some comparison with Chlorella. This may be partially due to the fact that both Chlorella and Spirulina are algae.

During the period from April through June 1977 it was widely reported in the papers that twenty-three people in the country had been discovered to be suffering from hypersensitivity to light and dermatitis (skin inflammation resulting from light hypersensitivity) caused by Chlorella and that eighteeen of these victims lived in the Tokyo Metropolitan area.

A recent issue of the *Japan Agricultural Chemistry Journal* (Vol. 53, No. 2) reported on this Chlorella poisoning event and its aftermath in the following manner.

"There is no precedent for a poisoning incident of this sort in people. Everyone was surprised, the consumers of Chlorella, the manufacturers, the doctors and the supervisory government agencies. The production of Chlorella as a health food, after some up and downs, had generally expanded in an orderly fashion, and now without rhyme or reason it was dealt a mortal blow. The over 200 Chlorella products which had been so popular in Japan were cut to half that number almost overnight. In this disaster Taiwan suffered most since they had increased their production (and production facilities) of Chlorella at the insistence of the Japanese merchants. Just when they were able to deliver in the quantity requested they were told that no one wanted to buy.

"As the investigation progressed it became clear that no abnormalities could be found in the 11 company products and 14 test samples other than the particular one which caused the incident, whether these were Chlorella drinks, powder or tablets.

"Recently the Food Products Department of the National Institute of Hygienic Sciences, the Food Hygiene Section of the Tokyo Metropolitan Health Institute and the manufacturer published the results of follow-up research designed to clarify the cause of this incident and to insure that there would not be a recurrence. The tests showed that in the process of manufacturing Chlorella products chlorophyll degraders (decomposers) were formed through the action of chlorophyllase and the like which remained in the original Chlorella. It was ascertained that the pheophorbide in those degraders was the substance responsible for causing hypersensitivity in people."

It was this food poisoning incident which prompted the general consumer's drifting away from Chlorella. The poisoning incident involving K Chlorella was the first to have received such wide-scale media coverage but there were a fairly large number of incidents of adverse effects which did not come into public view. There is a body of data gathered by the National Life Center. According to their figures, of the 135 cases of complaints about side effects brought to the Center during the three-year period 1975 through 1977 Chlorella topped the list with 45 cases.

If one looks at the nature of the adverse effects one finds 4 cases of diarrhea, vomiting and stomach pain; 4 cases of dizziness, heart palpitations and headaches; 11 cases of eczema and dermatitis as well as 9 other cases. There were also 8 cases related to K

Chlorella. Concerning the adverse effects connected with K Chlorella, it was shown that the cause was pheophorbide and further that the effects were restricted to the product manufactured by one company during a certain specific time period only.

According to animal experiments pheophorbide will cause skin damage such as eczema and the skin breaking out with sores when it is exposed to light. The fact that 11 of the 45 Chlorella victims sent to the Center had dermatitis or eczema shows that this particular brand of Chlorella contained a substance which caused photosensitive skin inflammation.

The age of Chlorella is over

The Center, which took these facts quite seriously, issued the following report in denying Chlorella food status (status as a product fit for human consumption as a food).

"Chlorella first attracted general interest just after the Second World War when food supplies were still inadequate. The fact that its protein content is quite large when compared with other vegetable food products was undoubtedly one of the reasons for its popularity, and certainly an analysis shows that it is a splendid protein source. But having a high protein content and being able to take full advantage of that content are not necessarily positively correlated. In Chlorella's case the protein is locked within a tough cellular membrane and thus it has a low rate of digestion. Thus there have appeared recently many techniques designed to break down the membrane and increase the digestibility or usability of Chlorella. Yet Chlorella no longer seems to be all that important as a protein source now that people can freely choose among a variety of protein food products.

"On the other hand, there are people who claim that Chlorella's effectiveness resides precisely in that tough membrane. The explanation is somewhat figurative but the gist is that since the membrane is hard to digest it acts in the body just like vegetable fiber. However if that were the source of its benefits it would be far more cost effective to simply eat the fiber of vegetables which were far less expensive.

"There may well be other useful and effective components of Chlorella but as yet there is no scientifically reliable data to explain or verify this."

Until this time the major sales point for Chlorella was its being a high protein food product. With this report, however, it became clear that no matter how high the protein content it had no food value if it could not be digested and absorbed in the body. Furthermore, the difficulty concerning the low digestion rate was a problem with the Chlorella itself, not something external.

This had already been pointed out by a number of scientists:

"Because it has a tough cellular membrane chlorella is extremely hard to digest. This is certainly a defect with respect to its usefulness as a food product and may on occasion raise questions about its use even as animal feed."
(*Food Industry*, Vol. 17, No. 4, Professor Ryukei Okawa, Fermentation Engineering Department, School of Engineering, Osaka University)

"As a cause for chlorella's indigestibility there is the question of the membrane wall of the chlorella cells and based on animal experiments there is also the question of inhibitive effects of the pigment chlorophyll or chlorophyll lipoprotein which exist in the chlorella cells."
(*Nutrition & Food Supply*) (Eigo to Shokuryo Vol. 30, No. 2 Aisateru Mitsuda, et al)

In the face of such criticism the manufacturers of chlorella brought out for sale a variety of Chlorella in which the cellular membrane was broken down and which was easy to absorb. But without the membrane performing the function of edible fibers in the diet, this Chlorella is then no different from Spirulina except that it has less nutritional value than Spirulina (it is a cut below Spirulina in terms of its ingredients). This point is most accurately and directly made by Dr. Hideo Ebine, Chief of the Applied Microbiology Section of the National Food Research Institute of the Ministry of Agriculture and Forestry.

"The old but new, blue green spriulina is, in comparison with the previously developed green algae group including chlorella and scenedesmus, superior in terms of the alkalinity of its culturing medium, as well as the divisibility and fertility derived from the size of the organism itself. It must also be said to be superior in terms of its nutritional value and its safety."

(*Food Science*, #27)

Spirulina is nearly perfect in all aspects

In basic research by a number of universities and research organizations who were asked to test it in a variety of modes Spirulina has been demonstrated to be safe as a food product and not to have side effects like the light hypersensitivity which became a problem with K Chlorella or any deformity-producing properties. I can also say that my investigations yield the same conclusion.

It is said that there are over 200 companies in Japan which have styled themselves as "Health Food Product Manufacturers". However, thus far Spirulina is the *first of all the health food products* made by these manufacturers to be thoroughly tested for safety. Moreover, many universities are reporting very impressive data concerning Spirulina in clinical situations. The data reveals that with its use, an improvement in condition does occur (diseases are ameliorated). In other words there has been clear, concrete observation of a promotion of health due to taking this product.

Doesn't this kind of food truly deserve to be called a "health food"? By no stretch of the imagination can it be regarded in the same light as questionable and dangerous food products which masquerade as health foods. From the consumer's point of view, some organization like the Ministry of Health and Welfare which has control over administration of foodstuff should clearly define production quality standards for health food products and should also strengthen their oversight of the distribution of such products. Without such measures the ambiguous pattern of manufacturing a "food product" while selling a "medicinal product" will proliferate. This would not be conducive to protecting the health of our citizens. Food at least must preserve standards of health.

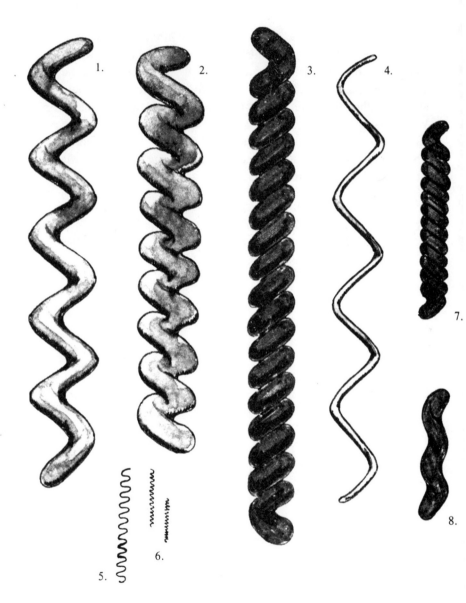

DIFFERENT TYPES OF SPIRULINA SPECIES

1. Spirulina platensis
2. Spirulina major
3. Spirulina princeps
4. Spirulina laxissima
5. Spirulina subtilissima
6. Spirulina caldaria
7. Spirulina curta
8. Spirulina spirulinoides

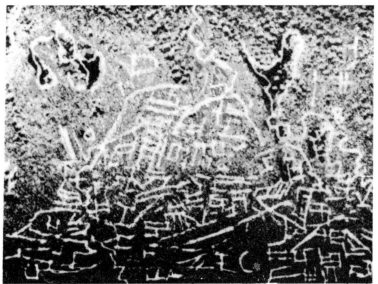

A radar image showing sophisticated system of Maya drainage canals that fed millions.

SPIRULINA—THE MAYAS SECRET

by Christopher Hills, Ph.D., D.Sc.

Recently it was discovered through space technology that the Mayas built a sophisticated canal network of so-called drainage canals that Mayanologists thought had transformed the swamplands into highly productive farmlands. Looking for archeological Mayan sites, researchers flew over thick jungles with a radar device designed originally to map the surface of Venus. The scanning device revealed a tremendous area patterned with a latticework of narrow waterways. Hacking through the rain forests of Guatemala and Belize and navigating through alligator-infested streams, the researchers found exactly what they suspected—a system of parallel canals that enabled the Mayas to feed a population of more than two million people. Like the Aztecs who used the alkaline lakes to grow Spirulina algae and mix this super-healthy protein with the starch of the maize corn, the Mayas built their system of growing tanks for the mass photosynthesis of algae.

Mystery continues to surround the Mayas who flourished as a highly intelligent civilization in the steamy jungles of Central America for over 1000 years before suddenly collapsing around 900 A.D. They erected huge cities, developed complex laws and systems of government, and spawned a priesthood which made incredible advances in mathematics and astronomy. But no one knew who fed their densely populated cities or how they suddenly disappeared. Most primitive farmers slash and burn the jungle trees to contribute minerals and ash to the soil, and after exhausting it, move on to new land leaving the makings of a desert behind them. Not so with the Mayas who excavated the earth onto the spaces between the canals and formed islands for drying the high yields of Spirulina algae cultivated in the long ponds and canals of brackish water. The mystery of how the Mayas declined so suddenly can now be explained. The complex system of waterways would need constant expert supervision of the algae cultures, because if they neglected to watch the seed cultures through drought or other concerns with warfare or calamity, then they would have nothing to keep the ponds blooming.

The Aztecs, who also grew Spirulina, were far away and possibly were hostile to the Mayas. Somehow the Mayas could not secure new seed cultures. After 1000 years of careful water control, their algoculturists and their aquaculture specialists may also have grown arrogant or over-confident, so that they would not know how to replace their lost seed culture in case of a wipe-out. Or perhaps they even tried to control the powers of the priests with the threat of strike, the destruction of the Spirulina culture through contamination or lack of nutrients, which would lead to an immediate collapse of the food supply for millions who had been kept alive for centuries by this superior method of aquaculture nutrition technology. The shape of the canals and the parallel ponds in the picture does not suggest efficient swamp drainage needed for corn culture as present-day archeologists have already theorized, but more resembles the Spirulina culture tanks of today.

The difference between the artificial culture of Spirulina in man-made canals and the wild algae which grows in the salt lakes of Mexico is the vulnerability to a sudden wipe-out of the crop. In artificial culture conditions there is always the chance that human error will cause something crucial to the maintenance of the crop to be forgotten, whereas in Lake Texcoco the crop grows prolifically whether anyone harvests it or not.

The phenomenon of a superior source of nutrition over a long period of time which could spawn such cultures as the Toltec and Mayan civilizations has its counterpart in the mastering of agriculture and husbandry techniques in the rich Nile basin of the ancient Egyptians which gave them the grains and animal proteins of a superior diet. However, the risk of collapse in land-based agriculture was not present in the evolution of 3000 years of Egyptian systems of government. While the skills of the Egyptians in their temperate Mediterranean climate were considerable, especially in the erection of buildings and sculpture, and showed some degree of scientific knowledge of astronomy, the Mayan system of government and its mathematics were incredibly advanced, even compared with present knowledge. A civilization which was based on Spirulina would not only stimulate good health in an inhospitable, hot jungle climate, but would enhance the vigor, energy and mental capacities of the people.

Spirulina, and blue-green algae generally, consists of many ingredients required for the manufacture of brain chemicals and hormones. The polypeptide chains of amino acids in such brain chemicals as enkephalins and endorphins and such hormones as insulin, needed for sugar metabolism for physical energy, and the production of dopamine needed for inducing natural inspirational and emotional religious states of consciousness, would all be present in a diet based on Spirulina. Being a very primitive organism, the Spirulina cell has no large vacuoles and the mitochondrion and the nucleus of its cells are not well-defined as they are in the less primitive higher plant cells. This allows for rapid photosynthesis and growth. Also, a large number of ribosomes are present in blue-green algae which enables it to synthesize proteins more rapidly. Some species of blue-green algae, suited to the hot jungle climates of Central America, can grow continuously at temperatures as high as 85°C (195°F) and although Spirulina can grow up to 45°C (112°F) it prefers the same growing temperature range as human blood cells. This preferential temperature may offer a link between Spirulina's efficient method of storing vitamins and pigments essential to rapid metabolism and its effectiveness when ingested by humans in their diet.

How Spirulina relates to energy metabolism

The metabolism of amino acids in the synthesis of glycogen and energy storage in the human body is dependent on there being a full spectrum of all amino acids available at the time of synthesis. If any one of them is missing then the body must make it or the particular protein cannot be made. Specific enzymes involved in the production of animal starches such as glycogen as well as enzymes which convert the sugars for energy release are also dependent on certain pigments in the liver and kidneys where the glycogen is made and where cell waste products are excreted in the urine. The role of amino acids in the production of the polypeptide brain chemicals and hormones is also crucial to the correct functioning of the endocrine system which produces such vital substances as insulin. Spirulina algae is the highest known source of many of the essential amino acids. (See chart on following page.)

The blue-green algae ribosomes synthesize the amino acids into proteins and store the granules of cyanophycean starch which is identical to the glycogen used as a storage product in animal and human cells. Animal starch usually differs from plant starch in being very highly branched and much more soluble in water. Glucose sugar cannot be stored in living cells because its molecules are small and they would leak out of cell membranes. The larger molecules of plant starch and glycogen will not pass through the cell plasma membrane. Glycogen is stored in animals and humans in the liver and muscles. Liver glycogen is converted to glucose by four enzymes. Glucose is then metabolized to CO_2 and water in order to release energy. Glucose is an absolutely indispensable component of blood. It is normally present in concentrations of about 0.1% by weight. The metabolic processes of brain cells require a constant supply of glucose for fuel. The complex synthesis of glucose involves the whole nervous system and its emotional hormones as well as biochemicals made in the liver, pancreas, pituitary and adrenal glands. Any athlete who wants to know how his muscles work must understand the metabolism of glucose sugars. The

The following percentages of amino acids are listed from the highest sources selected from over 350 ordinary foods.

Food	Glycine	Tryptophane	Methionine	Leucine	Cystine	Glutamic Acid
Spirulina	4.46	.97	2.12	4.56	.69	12.32
Meat	1.084	.204	.434	1.434	.221	2.649
Wheat	.855	.173	.214	.939	.307	4.375
Brown rice	.513	.081	.135	.646	.102	1.027
Bread	.301	.091	.142	.668	.200	2.952
Vegetable (Corn)	———	0.23	.072	.407	.062	———
Tofu	———	———	.081	———	.091	———
Fish	1.027	.185	.542	1.405	.250	2.369
Milk	.069	.049	.086	.344	.031	.819

Source: *Amino Acid Content of Foods*, by M.L. Orr and B.K. Watt, Household Economics Research Division, Institute of Home Economics Agricultural Research Service, U.S. Department of Agriculture, Home Economics Research Report No. 4, Washington, D.C., December 1957. Reviewed and approved for reprinting December 1968.

amazing wonder of Spirulina is that its glycogen content is immediately available to human metabolism. For joggers, athletes or people in need of more energy, glycogen gives a longer lasting energy rise than glucose. If you use glucose or fructose then you get a short rush which leaves you without the glycogen signal to the liver to provide more energy to your cells. Most vegetable starch or carbohydrates must go through the long process of reconstruction into glycogen before their nutrients are usable. Through panting and increasing your oxygen intake you have to build up a CO_2 signal in the blood system to get the glycogen going. Whereas taking Spirulina you send a signal to continue the production of glycogen immediately. Spirulina is the nearest vegetable life form to the animal world, and no other vegetable except the blue-green algae has this unique feature. Spirulina nutrients have the same profile as the human body and as a vegetable it can be considered an animal. This explains why Spirulina gives an immediate energy boost that is based on substantial nourishment that lasts.

Insulin is a hormone which has a direct effect on the metabolism of glucose, protein and lipids. It also stimulates the transport of glucose between the cells of the muscles and tissues and affects the utilization of sugar in the cells, including the liver, by converting glucose to glycogen and fat. Insulin also helps the oxidation of glucose into CO_2 and water. Insulin stimulates protein synthesis in the muscles, adipose tissue and liver. Hyperglycemia, or sugar diabetes, is a metabolic consequence of a diminished output or lower effectiveness of insulin production. Diabetes leads to decreased carbohydrate utilization and accelerated glucose levels which in turn results in osmotic increase in urine, sodium potassium losses and dehydration of cell water, and raises the levels of free fatty acids and lipids. The liver produces ketones which depress sensitivity to insulin and stimulate liver glucose, also inhibiting the protein synthesis of amino acids and converting them into glucose instead. If this continues without check the acid ketones accumulate in the blood and eventually exceed the rate of ketone excretion which in turn results in a decreased pH. This causes us to breathe faster to get rid of increased CO_2 but acidosis usually follows whenever we cannot get rid of these ketones through excretory processes. Ketosis is the result of inadequate insulin supply shown by symptoms of lassitude, thirst, frequent urination, a general feeling of being run down and loss of appetite. As ketosis progresses, acidosis develops until symptoms increase, with dizziness, deep breathing, nausea, vomiting and eventually diabetic coma. The urine then contains large amounts of glucose, acetone and diacetic acid.

Insulin metabolism is a key factor in protein synthesis of amino acids and the production of lipids. In the specification of Spirulina we can see that proteins amount to 70% and that total lipids amount to 7%. These lipids consist mainly of unsaturated fatty acid, practically all gamma linoleic acid. This acid has been considered the precursor of arachidic acid, a saturated fatty acid in the body, and represents about 20% of the total fats found in Spirulina. Many vitamins, minerals, and several pigments are also abundant compared with other vegetables and animal sources. Spirulina contains beta carotene (provitamin A) the B_1, B_2, B_6-B_{12} vitamins, a small amount of C, the E vitamin and an exceptional amount of Vitamin H or Biotin. The anemic factor in blood caused by lack of B_{12} is not found in Spirulina eaters because it contains the world's richest source of B_{12}, 250% more than the next highest source—beef liver.

The pigments in Spirulina such as carotene, xanthophyll, phycobilin and phycocyanine, porphyrin, phycoerythrin and several other chlorophyll pigments are important to our metabolic processes. Spirulina contains over 7% of its weight in phycocyanin as well as 1% in chlorophyll and 4% carotenoids. The phycobilin pigments have a pyrrole structure and contain the phycocyanobilin B_{12} vitamins as well as the blue phycobilin called phycocyanine and the red phycobilin called phycoerythrin.

Distantly related to the lipids are the tetrapyrroles or porphyrins which are certain pigments in plants and animals which are photosensitive and change color. The pyrrole molecule contains a skeleton of five atoms, four of which are carbon and one nitrogen, and the five are arranged in a ring. Four of these pyrrole rings joined together form into a tetrapyrrole structure which determines the color of chlorophyll, feces, birds' eggs, urine and blood. The straight chain skeleton shown below is chemically similar to bilirubin which is one of the breakdown products of hemoglobin in our blood. The cytochromes, which serve as hydrogen-carrying co-enzymes of plant and animal mitochondria, are closely related to the oxygen-transporting compounds in the blood of animals (hemes) and chlorophyll. The diagram shows the structure of these pigments.

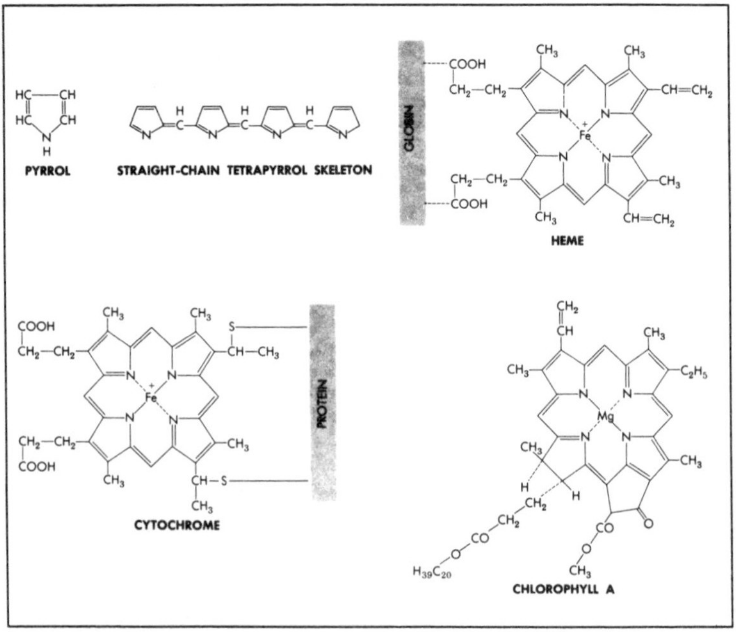

In fact, porphyrin's pyrrole molecule forms the basic structure and active nucleus of the pigments chlorophyll, hemoglobin and cytochromes. The cytochrome is a respiratory pigment occuring in animal and plant cells in the mitochondria that serve as energy storage batteries and electron carriers in biological oxidation of all living cells. These pigments in Spirulina are probably the most important pigments in the metabolism of cells in all vegetable and animal life and if we cannot obtain or eat them from those plants or animals which can synthesize them, it is certain that nutritional diseases will occur. Therefore, Spirulina is an excellent nutritional source of these vital pigments.

The Japanese have extracted vitamin K or phytonadione from Spirulina, a yellow liquid formed in the intestinal flora which assists coagulation of blood and clotting and triggers the liver to begin production of those proteins which act as anti-coagulants in the body. A pigment is any matter in animal or plant cells that colors and reflects light of certain wavelengths while absorbing light of other wavelengths. The normal color of the body, its organs, its blood and cells results from the pigments deposited in the tissues and the pigments carried in the blood bathing the tissues. The red and green bile pigments come from bilirubin and biliverdin which are produced in the liver to aid digestion and encourage enzyme production in the breaking down of amino acids in the intestines. Because red and green make black when they are equally mixed together, bile can appear black or dark brown as can Spirulina when the porphyrins and red phycoerythrins are dominating in the chlorophyll.

Spirulina contains the yellow/orange pigments cryptoxanthin and B carotene and several other carotenoids. Three of these can be converted naturally to vitamin A by the wall of the intestinal tract. One unit of vitamin A can be formed from two units of B carotene in this way. Vitamin A is not normally found in high quantities in vegetable products but only in mammals and salt-water fish. The RDA for vitamin A is 1000 international units of preformed vitamin A or 4000 international units of B carotene, but the AMA recommends 5000 international units. An international unit (I.U.) is defined as the activity of 0.6 micrograms of beta carotene. Fish livers contain high amounts of vitamin A by accumulating it through the food chain originating with algae. There is a large chemical company at present contemplating extracting carotene from Spirulina.

Athletes and joggers are interested in the performance of muscles and the respiration of the amino acids which make glycogen through pyruvic acid to CO_2 which is referred to as glycolysis. This process feeds into the citric acid cycle which is aided by ATP, a stored chemical energy in mitochondria in the muscles which helps to oxidate or convert the glycogen animal starch into glucose and muscle energy. It is possible to assist this process through vitamins. The same breaking down of amino acids takes place with proteins and is stored as glycogen in muscles to be used as energy and tissue building.

Because pyridoxine (vitamin B6) is a precursor of a co-enzyme serving as an NH2 (amino group) carrier in transaminations (transfer of one amino acid into another through enzyme reactions such as the citric acid cycle, alanine to pyruvic acid, and glutamic acid to a-ketoglutaric acid), it can be used in combination with Spirulina to enhance the metabolic processes of transferring the high percentage of amino acids in Spirulina to a much-needed protein or energy synthesis in the body. Biotin (vitamin H) becomes a CO_2-carrying enzyme in the oxidation of cells where the CO_2-fixing reactions of carbohydrates can be given longer carbon chains and this enzyme may also assist in eliminating the waste products of carbohydrate energy metabolism.

Another interesting factor in Spirulina is its effect upon appetite. Either it is so concentrated that the body signals a satisfaction feeling from the digestive tract where Spirulina has a remarkable 85% digestibility or it controls hunger and appetite from the hypothalamus centers in the brain. It is known that the hunger center and the satiety center react to glucose levels in the blood so Spirulina may have some unknown effects on sugar metabolism or alternatively work directly on the brain hormone balances. It is here where the editor believes we must look for Spirulina's remarkable effects on our state of mind as well as our health.

SPIRULINA AS
NUTRITION FOR THE BRAIN

by Christopher Hills, Ph.D., D.Sc.

There is increasing awareness of the role of primitive natural vegetable organisms, such as microalgae which contain high amounts of vitamins and amino acids in the correction of nutrition imbalances. This book, *The Secrets of Spirulina*, recently published in Japan by doctors researching the medical effects of Spirulina and edited in English by me, deals with the common diseases of a civilized society like Japan. But my interest in Spirulina is more in the prevention of disease and the gaining of super health and rejuvenation. Although the general health of Americans and Europeans is no better than the Japanese, and reports of spontaneous results from people suffering from long-term problems have poured in from users of Spirulina from all over the world who have taken the Spirulina algae purely for nutritional reasons, the interesting part of the "Spirulina secret" for myself is the remarkable effects of this vegetable plankton on our state of consciousness particularly while fasting on nothing else. A more detailed program is now being undertaken to discover why most people feel increased energy and clarity of mind after taking the Spirulina as a vitamin supplement.

The role of vitamins in superhealth is being questioned by athletes who are now trying a great deal of other nutrients in their search for perfect metabolism. They are turning to natural sources of energy rather than refined casein proteins and synthetic vitamins. Combinations of Spirulina with niacin, pyridoxine and calcium gluconate aid athletes in circulation, and may, according to the Japanese, activate production of hormones, especially adrenalin and insulin as well as increase the efficiency of the nervous system and supply glycogen energy to the muscles.

Vitamins are organic chemicals which are present in foods in very small amounts. They are essential for good health. If any vitamin is missing from our diet, a specific disease will occur because a vitamin cannot be made by our body. Hormones and brain chemicals are the same organic chemicals as vitamins but the difference is that they are made by our body. If our normal body chemistry does not produce these certain brain chemicals or hormones adequately, then various symptoms and diseases occur. Many people think of themselves as different from animals such as elephants or snails or whales, but in most ways the proteins of animal cells are made up of the same amino acids, vitamins and hormones only in different proportions.

The unity of nature is profound. By eating vegetables and animal proteins we obtain the amino acids and vitamins which they have stored in their cells. Vitamin C is a vitamin to human bodies but a hormone in other animals because they can produce it within their bodies whereas humans do not. In the same way, amino acids are organic chemicals which are produced by metabolic processes within the body and can be considered the building blocks of protein and cell manufacture. However, there are eight essential amino acids which cannot be synthesized by our body and they must be obtained, like vitamins, by eating those foods, either plants or animals, which can synthesize them. If our normal metabolic processes cannot synthesize enough of the amino acids that we do produce within ourselves the effect of a shortage of these so-called non-essential amino acids will be the same as a shortage of the eight essential ones.

The metabolic processes of nutrition and the building of proteins in the healthy cell is not completely understood by modern science, even though many specific effects of vitamins and the primary role of hormones are now known. Enzymes present in the human body vary with each individual and many vitamins are used by these enzymes to fabricate the biochemicals we need for proper amino acid protein synthesis within the cell. A vitamin is often used by the enzymes to join certain kinds of molecules together in the production of a long chain of chemical reactions. These complicated chemicals, like the long molecules of the endorphins and polypeptides made in the brain, are the products of enzymes which are themselves large protein molecules which are formed in the body out of the amino acids we eat. When a vitamin is absent the body's cell machinery and its enzyme production begins to break down and then we cannot feel healthy and experience that state of well-being which we experienced in youth.

To feel healthier and happier we must not only extract nutrients from what we eat but also assimilate them through proper digestion. If our digestive processes are inefficient the vitamins and organic amino acids cannot be assimilated. Not only does the body require efficient assimilation of proteins, amino acids and vitamins, but there must be also good elimination, because it is through the intestine and its remarkable cells that we assimilate.

There is an increasing body of medical opinion which is leaning towards the natural ways of assimilating vitamins rather than administering large doses of synthetic vitamins as if they were drugs. The highly assimilated natural foods, such as Spirulina, have incredibly long strings of amino acids of several kinds which are the building blocks for living cells. The proteins of Spirulina are 80–85% assimilated as against 20% for beef protein. Also Spirulina is 65–71% protein as against beef which is about 18%. Our digestive tract takes all proteins from whatever source and breaks them down into amino acids which are passed on to the cells as nutrients. In order for cells to build a particular protein, all the required amino acids must be available to them at the same time. If one is missing in the food we eat then that protein molecule cannot be synthesized. These amino acids do not stay around in the body until the next day because they are highly unstable in the body and will be snatched by other cells and used for building other proteins or burnt away as energy or excreted. The job of building a particular protein cannot wait until tomorrow because the missing amino acids which come in tomorrow's meals will not find yesterday's amino acids still in the body. They are not saved until the next meal, so it becomes important that food is not only complete with all essential amino acids but that any missing amino acid which we find difficulty in producing through internal metabolism must also be supplied. Amino acids react together to form peptide bonds and form an amide linkage. Ingestion of certain amino acids into the hydrochloric acid of the stomach such as L-glutamine and asparagine will de-aminate by hydrolysis to glutamic acid and aspartic acids, so there is no point in putting the former into foods when you can put the latter which are much cheaper to produce. The breaking of the peptide bond is called hydrolysis because water is added to the amino acid molecule. Most amino acids form long chains or polymers which are called polypeptides.

The naming of certain amino acids as essential is a misnomer because all the amino acids produced by the body and those taken in from foods are essential to proper metabolism. The long chains of brain chemicals are proteins made up of polypeptides such as the diagram below of Methionine enkephalin:

Met-ENKEPHALIN

L-Glutamic acid function is of major importance in brain metabolism. A so-called non-essential amino acid which is produced within the body and converted to L-Glutamine, the natural Glutamic acid, serves primarily as brain fuel along with the Glucose which is formed out of our foods.

AMINO ACID STRUCTURE

The amino acid structures are very similar to other important nutritive metabolites which enter the Krebs citric acid cycle, such as Pyruvic acid. Alanine and Glutamic acid and Aspartic acid are oxydized and enter directly into the citric acid cycle.

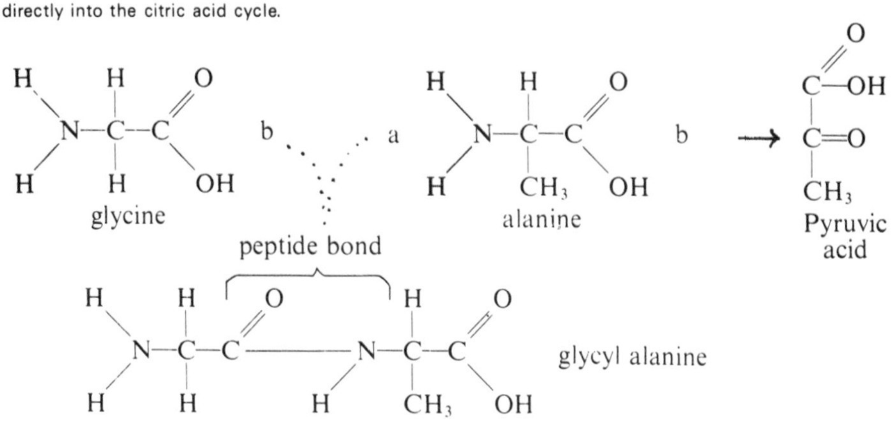

glycine

peptide bond

alanine

Pyruvic acid

glycyl alanine

The structural formulas of the amino acids Glycine and Alanine, showing (a) the amino group and (b) the acid (carboxyl) group. These may be joined by a peptide bond to form Glycylalanine by the removal of water.

Standard base structure of all amino acids is shown at right. The lower portion of the following diagrams illustrates the unique characteristics of each individual amino acid.

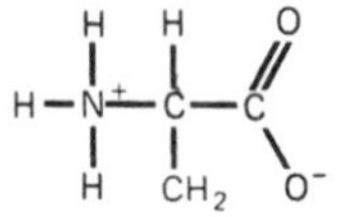

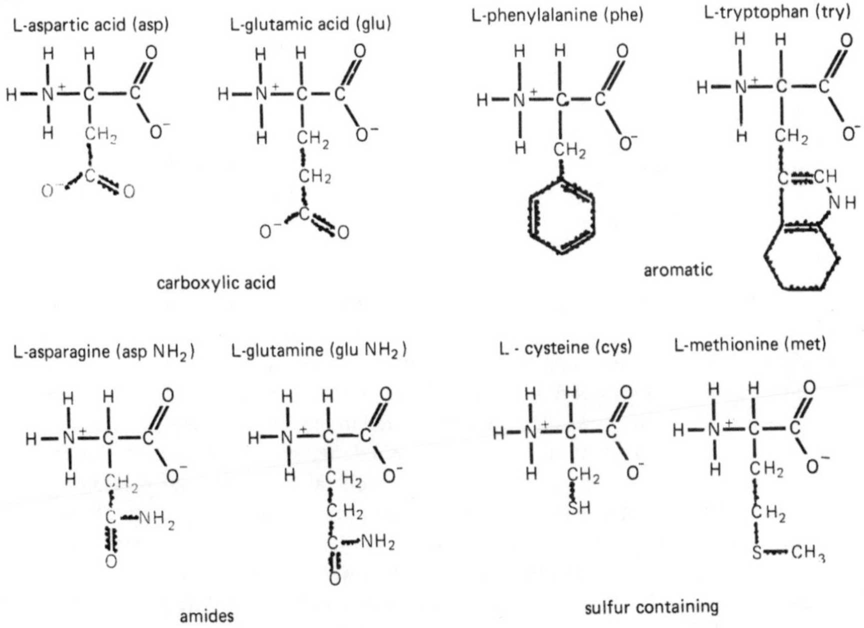

L-aspartic acid (asp)   L-glutamic acid (glu)

carboxylic acid

L-phenylalanine (phe)   L-tryptophan (try)

aromatic

L-asparagine (asp NH₂)   L-glutamine (glu NH₂)

amides

L - cysteine (cys)   L-methionine (met)

sulfur containing

Dotted lower portions of the above diagrams represent each characteristic difference between the bases and the amino acids.

Glutamic acid has the ability to pick up excess Ammonia and be converted into L-Glutamine because it only differs in structure by the combination of the nitrogen molecule, and oxygen and hydrogen molecules as follows:

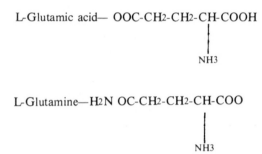

The relationship between Glutamic acid and Glucose goes much farther than their brain fuel interaction. For instance, Glutamic acid helps to restore to consciousness hypoglycemia (low blood sugar) patients suffering from insulin shock or coma, at a lower level of blood sugar than when glucose is used alone as an injection. Glutamic acid metabolism in the brain is utilized by certain enzymes in the brain to regulate brain cell activity and by-passes the normal machinery of the body for fuel through glucose-energy-ATP production.

L-Glutamine has also been used in studies of alcoholism, has shortened the healing time of ulcers and has been recommended to fight fatigue, depression and impotence in doses of 1000 mg. three times a day. But L-Glutamine has the well-known hydrolysis effect in the stomach which reduces it to L-Glutamic acid and therefore makes it difficult to get L-Glutamine into the blood and directly to the brain. The body makes its own L-Glutamine from L-Glutamic acid and since it is L-Glutamic acid which is needed by the brain anyway there is not much point in ingesting L-Glutamine.

There are some people today recommending low protein diets and high carbohydrates of the complex starches. This is because they believe that Americans eat too much protein. However, this is a misunderstanding of correct metabolism. It does not matter to the body over long periods whether you eat proteins or starches because all are converted in the body into amino acids and then into glycogen for storage in the cells. What matters is a balance between the complex sugars and the proteins. Spirulina itself can be made to grow into 70% carbohydrate polysaccharides or 70% protein merely by changing its pH and depriving it of nitrogen. The human body is similar and there is new evidence to suggest that it does not matter whether weight watchers eat protein or complex carbohydrates. The main point in dieting is to avoid energy storage in fats and glycogen by limiting intake of simple sugars and fats.

Anyone who is interested in efficient metabolism must study the relationship between the polypeptides and the production of insulin which controls the levels of sugars delivered to the cells for the purpose of energy use. The same applies to other hormones manufactured internally. But insulin balance with Spirulina has been studied extensively by the Japanese. Monosaccharides such as glucose and fructose and disaccharides such as sucrose are the basic materials of energy exchanges in nature. With sugar, the bond joining two monosaccharides is created by a reaction which eliminates water from the crystals. When the sugar bond is broken by the addition of water molecules the reverse process of hydrolysis takes place.

All these simple sugars are synthesized in green plants and algae by the process of photosynthesis, by splitting carbon dioxide from water and using light rays as the energy source. The cell then releases chemical energy stored in them by the breakdown of these carbohydrates. When a number of monosaccharides are attached together they form such polysaccharides as starch, glycogen and cellulose. For example, glycogen is formed out of thousands of glucose residues and represents in animal and human cells an efficient storage device which can always break down those large carbohydrate glycogen molecules whenever the cell needs energy. Starch is the equivalent carbohydrate energy storage device of plant cells. Spirulina is high in glycogen but low in starch.

Insulin is made of two different polypeptide chains held together by di-sulphide bonds which are formed by the side chains of two sulphurs containing cysteine residues. Hence the importance of a methylating agent such as L-cysteine methylester HCl in sugar metabolism should be fully researched in nutrition as well as the peptide bonds which are present between other amino acids in Spirulina and the regular foods we eat.

Another important ingredient of Spirulina in the diet is the presence of about 4000 mg/kg of carotene of several kinds. Carotenoids cannot be manufactured in the bodies of animals and humans but they play an important role in nutrition. Carotene is one of the pigments synthesized by plants which are necessary for the process of photosynthesis. Vitamin A obtained from natural sources as pro vitamin A is non-toxic and is necessary for vision. Other pigments such as phycobilin (protein bond pigments with open chain molecules), phycocyanin (a blue phycobilin) and cyancobalamin (Vit. B12) are all plentiful in Spirulina.

Another pigment which may also account for Spirulina's remarkable effects is porphyrin, a red pigmented compound with cyclic tetra-pyrrole structure in which four pyrrole rings are joined together by their carbon atoms. Porphyrin forms the active nucleus of chlorophyll and hemoglobin. The polypyrrole structure of B12 which contains the anti-anemia factor may be related since the hemoglobin molecule is the oxygen-carrying iron molecule of red blood cells which helps to oxidize the metabolites in the cell.

Spirulina is a vitamin food which is complete and concentrated. By combining its 85% digestibility and its vast profile of vitamins and amino acids with specific additions of natural amino acids we can find out, one by one, through experimenting with these natural products in our own bodies, which of the particular amino acids we may be lacking. Spirulina by itself has been given to all kinds of people in Japan with medical complaints which would place it in the eyes of the FDA as a drug. Spontaneously people have reported a number of remissions of chronic and acute conditions which are obviously nutritionally caused. FDA law prohibits making any claims for this product in the USA, but the recent book published in Japan by fifteen medical doctors shows that there are medical effects, which would have to be validated in the USA all over again to gain FDA approval. But Spirulina, taken as a vitamin supplement, is a safe, natural product which has been eaten for centuries by Aztecs and Africans and therefore we are able to recommend nutritionally using any amount of it without causing any toxicity. Tests with rats in Japan reveal that Spirulina is completely non-toxic.

SUMMARY OF BRAIN HORMONES
AND THEIR AMINO ACID STRUCTURE

ENKEPHALIN

Type: neuropeptide (short chain of amino acids) Met and Leu types (Methionine) (Leucine)
Function: ● migrates across the floor of the third ventricle, then triggers the hypothalamus which in turn triggers the pineal gland to activate the higher centers of the brain. (See author's book *Rise of the Phoenix*, pages 207-613, on the seven levels of brain function.) ● Enkephalin is a natural pain killer and tranquilizer like morphine.
Origin: released by pituitary.

Met-ENKEPHALIN

Tyr Gly Gly Phe Met

Tyr Gly Gly Phe Leu

Leu-ENKEPHALIN

ENDORPHIN

Type: B-ENDORPHIN
Function: ● helps memory and concentration, ● reduces anxiety, counters depression. ● A pain killer (natural opiate).
Origin: secreted in third ventricle.

β--ENDORPHIN

DOPAMINE

Type: mono-amine transmitter
Location: Substantia nigra and ventral tegmentum regions of brain (mid-brain)
Function: ● projected to forebrain—regulates emotional response ● determinate in corpus striatum (complex movements) ● degeneration of dopamine fibres — Parkinson's disease; excess dopamine — Schizophrenia

DOPAMINE

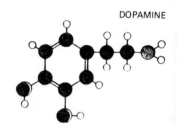

MELATONIN

Origin: pineal gland

Function: ● governs rhythmic functions of brain ● ultraviolet light stimulates melatonin production which stimulates tanning of skin, ● also stimulates sex gland ● when eyes closed, melatonin channeled into brain instead of periphery thus activating intuitive centers

MELATONIN

$CH_3 - O$

$CH_2CHN - C - CH_3$

GABA
gamma-aminobutyric acid

Type: amino acid

Location: manufactured in brain and spinal cord

Function: ● inhibitory transmitter ● a deficit of GABA may be involved in Huntington's Chorea ● may be involved in anti-anxiety ● does not cross blood-brain barrier

GABA

SUBSTANCE P

Type: neuropeptides (short chain of amino acids)

Function: ● transmitter of brain signals carried by sensory nerves into spinal cord and then relayed to brain ● Substance P may be suppressed by endorphins ● Sub. P tends to excite neurons ● Sub P stimulates Dopamine

SUBSTANCE P

(Arg)(Pro)(Lys)(Pro)(Gln)(Gln)(Phe)(Phe)(Gly)(Leu)(Met) NH₂

NOREPINEPHRINE

Type: monoamine (transmitter)

Location: ● norepinephrine neurons are projected to cerebellum, forebrain and located also in brain stem ● released by adrenal medulla

Function: ● maintenance of wakefulness, ● brain system of reward ● in dreaming sleep ● regulation of mood

NOREPINEPHRINE

OXYTOCIN

Type: ● neuropeptide (short chain of amino acids)

Origin: posterior pituitary

Function: ● affects uterus—propels sperm into uterus and fetus from uterus

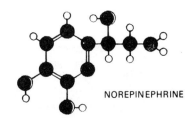

OXYTOCIN

(Ile)(Tyr)(Cys)
(Gln)(Asn)(Cys)(Pro)(Leu)(Gly) NH₂

ACTH (Adrenocorticotrophin) Adrenal Cortical Stimulating Hormone

Type: neuropeptide hormone **Origin:** anterior pituitary **Function:** ● essential for normal development & functional activity of adrenal cortex ● stimulates production of cortisone and other adrenocortical hormones

ACTH (CORTICOTROPIN)

(Ser)(Tyr)(Ser)(Met)(Glu)(His)(Phe)(Arg)(Tyr)(Gly)(Lys)(Pro)(Val)(Gly)(Lys)(Lys)(Arg)(Arg)(Pro)(Val)(Lys)(Val)(Tyr)

(Pro)(Asp)(Gly)(Ala)(Glu)(Asp)(Glu)(Leu)(Ala)(Glu)(Ala)(Phe)(Pro)(Leu)(Glu)(Phe)

SEROTONIN

Type: similar to LSD in structure
Origin: pineal gland, concentrated in Raphe nuclei region of brain
Function: ● neural inhibitor, function dependent on interaction of enzymes and hormones ● deep sleep induced by action on reticular activating system; temperature regulation and sensory perception ● dilates blood vessels in brain ● light stimulates serotonin production ● serotonin production is coupled with ionization of fluids in 3rd ventricle ● does not cross blood-brain barrier ● found in bananas, plums, and figs

SEROTONIN

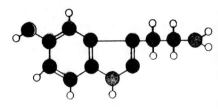

SOMATOTROPHIN (STH)
Pituitary Growth Hormone (GH)

Type & Structure: ● a protein ● molecular weight = 21,500 ● has phenylalanine as both N-terminal and C-terminal amino acids
Origin: anterior pituitary
Function: ● growth of bones ● retention of nitrogen ● secretion of milk from mammary gland

LUTEINIZING HORMONE (LH)
ICSH (in male)—interstitial cell stimulating hormon

Structure: a glycoprotein ● molecular weight = 25,000
Type: one of three gonadotrophins
Origin: anterior pituitary
Function: ● in male: stimulates production o testerone ● in female: development of follicle int corpus luteum.

In conclusion, we might mention that there is at least one patent in Japan for using the porphyrins obtained from Spirulina for arresting cancer growth. This will no doubt create a great deal of interest amongst doctors when the patent is recorded over here in the USA. People interested in Spirulina can write to me, Dr. Christopher Hills (Ph.d., D.Sc.) President, Microalgae International Union, P.O. Box 644, Boulder Creek, CA 95006.

Ala	ALANINE	Leu	LEUCINE
Arg	ARGININE	Lys	LYSINE
Asn	ASPARAGINE	Met	METHIONINE
Asp	ASPARTIC ACID	Phe	PHENYLALANINE
Cys	CYSTEINE	Pro	PROLINE
Gln	GLUTAMINE	Ser	SERINE
Glu	GLUTAMIC ACID	Thr	THREONINE
Gly	GLYCINE	Trp	TRYPTOPHAN
His	HISTIDINE	Tyr	TYROSINE
Ile	ISOLEUCINE	Val	VALINE

APPENDIX

How to obtain Spirulina

Spirulina is available both as a food supplement and as animal feed. The Spirulina developed by Greater Japan Chemical Ink Industries, Inc. (DIC) is available in Japan under the following labels at pharmacies and drug counters throughout the country.

"Linagreen", Sankyo Trading Co., 3-5-5 Katsudoki, Chuo-ku, Tokyo, Tel: (03) 531-6261

"Hei-liena", Mannan Foods, Inc., Rigen Building #2, 2-10-2 Kyobashi, Chuo-ku, Tokyo, Tel: (03) 564-6071 (A member of the Dolphin Trademark Store Chain)

"Spirulina Kayaku", Kayaku Kosebusabitsu Kenkyuuo, Inc., 2-16-23, Tel: (03) 987-2101

"Spirulina C", Toyo Rassbau Seiyaku (Pacific Russian Pharmaceuticals, Inc.) Kyodo Building, 2-5 Nihonbashi Honeko, Chuo-ku, Tokyo, Tel: (03) 270-1630

"Professional Metabolics"—a division of Aquaculture Nutrition Products Co.—sells the Mexican quality grown in Lake Texcoco. 22376 Thunderbird Place, Hayward, Calif. 94545. Tel: (408) 338-4827

The official USA Distributor for the Mexican producers is Dr. Christopher Hills, who pioneered the introduction of microalgae as a future food over the last twelve years along with Dr. Hiroshi Nakamura.
Tel: (408) 338-2544

Light Force Spirulina Company, P.O. Box N, 13190 Central Ave., Boulder Creek, Calif. 95006. Tel: (408) 338-4820. *Light Force* sells vitamin supplements by direct sales similar to the Shaklee and Amway system **in the USA.**

Further reading on Spirulina . . .

FOOD FROM SUNLIGHT
Christopher Hills and Hiroshi Nakamura

Of all the problems facing our planet hunger is one of the most perplexing and saddening. Starvation is a reality for perhaps two-thirds of the earth's people, and each day we seem to hear of famine hitting yet another part of the globe. At last there is a solution: microalgae. *Food From Sunlight* tells every aspect of its potential to feed the world: how to grow algae, facts and figures about the amazing nutritional benefits of Chlorella and Spirulina, two superior strains, and how to bring our deserts and exhausted lands back into productive use. Algae is an excellent source of energy and some strains even thrive on pollution. Every survivalist will want to get his hands on this invaluable book.

Well illustrated, 384 pp., $14.95

REJUVENATING THE BODY
Through Fasting with Spirulina Plankton
Christopher Hills, Ph.D., D.Sc.

The world's newest "super" food has actually been known to the Aztec and African cultures for centuries. In Japan it is a staple part of the diet and is even fed to prize-winning fish. An 85-year-old man has lived on nothing else for the past 15 years. What is it? Spirulina Plankton, the total food for health, rejuvenation and survival. *Rejuvenating the Body* describes practical uses for Spirulina, the highest form of natural vegetable protein available on this planet. Thousands of people are discovering the benefits of this remarkable food and nutritional supplement. *Rejuvenating the Body* contains a complete, easy-to-follow program to cleanse our bodies and bring back vigor and the blush of health.

45,000 copies of this book are now in print.

Illustrated, 64 pp, $2.50

INDEX

A

abrocinine: 93
acidity: 46-47
Akatsuka, Prof. Kenichi: 14, 127
alcohol: 73, 82-83, 86-87
algae (see also Spirulina): 1-9, 26, 34, 36-41, 49, 164-69, 197
alkalinity: 46-47
American Journal of Medicine: 153
amino acids: 41, 43, 81, 83, 85, 199, 200, 201, 203, 204-208, 210-212
anemia: 47, 67-72
Animal Breeding Research Center: 139
animal experimentation: 1, 9, 129-31, 136-37, 141-45
Animal Husbandry Research Institute: 41, 141
asthenopia: 103

B

baldness (see "circular depilation")
behavior and learning: 144
Behcet's Disease: 107
bilirubin: 68, 203
birth defects: 9, 140-45
blood: 4, 60, 64, 67, 70, 74-75, 82, 136, 137, 175, 201-204
blood sugar: 60, 64, 65, 66, 81, 90, 103, 104
bones: 141, 144
brain: 198, 199, 204-212

C

Caesarean section: 143
Calvin, Prof.: 180
Cancer: 87
caracol pond: 32, 164, 166
carbohydrates: 42, 81
Carnegie Foundation: 51
cataracts: 99, 100, 101, 106
Central Food Technology Research Center: 168
central nervous system: 130
Centre House: 2, 28
Chad: 26, 29
Chlorella: 2, 3, 6, 14, 43, 50-54, 135, 165, 167, 172, 190-94
Chlorella Industries: 52

Chlorella International Union: 28
chlorophyll: 22, 42, 76, 134, 172-181, 202, 203, 204
chloroplast: 172-74, 180
cholesterol: 74-75
chromoplast: 172-174
circular depilation: 124-126
cirrhosis of the liver: 16, 58, 75, 80, 81, 83-85
Clement, Prof.: 164, 165
coloring agents: 42, 43
constipation: 120
corpuscles: 67-68

D

Delbruch, Prof. M.: 49
Denen Chofu Clinic: 123
dermatitis: 14
detoxification: 82
Deurben: 29
diabetes: 16, 58-66, 103
diarrhea: 94, 95
diet: 62, 64, 68, 69, 70, 93, 95, 99, 100, 114, 116-18, 156-62
digestion: 14, 90-92, 179, 192-93
drugs: 9, 14, 140
duodenum: 90

E

Ebine, Prof. Hideo: 165, 194
enzymes: 90-91, 199, 203, 204
Ethiopia: 27, 34, 36, 37, 38
exercise: 111-12
Exodus: 7-8
eye disease: 16, 98-108
fasting: 9

F

fasting: 9
fats: 42, 83
FDA: 1, 13, 210
fertility: 142
Food from Sunlight: 2
French National Petroleum Research Center: 27
Fujii, Dr. Naoharu: 147

G

gastritis: 76-77, 119, 179
gastroptosis: 120
Germany: 49, 50
glaucoma: 101
glucose: 60, 65, 81, 199, 201, 203, 208
glutamic acid: 206-208
glycogen: 60, 81, 199-201, 203, 205, 209
Goto, Prof. Yuichiro: 184
Gottingen University: 50
Greater Japan Chemical Ink Industries, Inc.: 9, 37, 40, 41, 56, 99, 141, 184
"green blood": 22, 172-181

H

hair (see also "circular depilation"): 123-25
Harada, Isao: 112
Harada's Disease: 102, 107
Hashimoto, Prof. Michio: 134
Hauser Food Products: 185-86
health foods (see also "natural foods"): 128-29, 131, 184-95
hematocrit level: 136
hemoglobin: 4, 67, 136, 175-76, 203
hemorrhaging: 105, 106, 107
hepatitis: 71-76, 94, 119
Herden, Prof.: 50
high blood pressure: 100
Hills, Dr. Christopher: 34
Hippocrates: 20
hormones: 188-189, 198, 199, 205, 210-212
hydroureterites: 144
hyper-photosensitivity: 136

I

"Impossibility Thinkers": 5-9
inflammation: 36, 91, 92, 102
insulin: 59, 62, 90, 198, 199, 201, 205, 209
International Christian University: 165
iron: 68, 69, 70
Iwao, Hiroyuki: 185

J

Japan Chlorella Research Institute: 51, 52
Japan Dietary Association: 51
Japanese Spirulina Development Committee: 6
Joslyn, Prof.: 66

K

Kawamura Institute for Physical and Chemical Research: 184
Keio University Medical School: 184
Koryama Women's University: 14, 133
Kuroda, Dr.: 113
Kyoto Medical College: 89

L

Lake Aranguadi: 27, 35, 36, 37
Lake Chad: 3, 164
Lake Johann: 29
Lake Texcoco: 3, 30, 198
Lake Totalcingo: 30
leucoma: 101
leucoplast: 172, 74
light
hypersensitivity to: 134
Lindner, Prof.: 49
liver: 59, 70, 73, 74, 80-88, 199, 201, 203
longevity rate: 149-50, 157

M

Matsui, Toru: 5
Mayans: 197-98
Meiji University College of Pharmacology: 14
melanin: 125
metabolism: 198, 199, 201, 202, 204-205, 209
Mexico: 1, 2, 3, 13, 164-67
microalgae (see also "algae", "Spirulina"): 2-3, 48, 51
Microalgae International Union: 28, 34
Migushima, Hiroshi: 188
Ministry of Agriculture and Forestry: 165, 185

Ministry of Health and Welfare: 84, 118, 185, 195
Minot: 70
modern society: 112-16, 117-18, 128, 154, 158
Molecular Corrective Medicine: 48
mutations: 143
myopia: 105, 106
myopic astigmatism: 106

N

Nakamura, Prof. Hiroshi: 2, 6, 25, 28, 118, 165
Nakao, Sasuke: 168
National (Citizen's) Nutrition Survey: 117
National Food Research Institute: 194
National Institute of Hygienic Sciences: 135, 191
National Institute of Nutrition: 185
National Life Center: 191
natural foods (see also "health foods"): 22-24, 140
nausea: 94

O

obesity: 62, 103, 104
orthomolecular medicine: 154, 155, 161
oxygen: 46, 67, 68
pain: 95, 119, 120
pancreas: 90-96
pancreatitis: 90, 91-96
parturition: 142
Pateck: 85
Pauling, Linus: 48, 154, 156, 157, 158
peripheral nervous system: 129-30
Pharmaceutical University College of Meiji: 127
photosynthesis: 176, 181
phycocyanine: 42, 136, 137, 202
plankton: 4
pollution: 20-21, 22
porphyrin: 3, 174, 175-176, 202, 203, 209
portal veins: 80, 81
"Possibility Thinkers": 5-9

potassium: 119, 136, 137
processed foods: 115
protein: 2, 41, 42, 72-73, 74, 81, 83, 85, 161, 167, 168, 199, 201, 205, 208
pseudo-myopia: 103, 104
pure culturing: 37-38
pyrrole: 3, 174, 175, 202, 203, 209

R

retinal angiosclerosis: 100
retinitis: 100
rhodotorula: 49

S

Sakai, Dr. Tomokichi: 109
Saitama Medical College: 56
Salt: 27, 29, 30, 31, 35, 36, 37
2nd International Conference on Microbiological Protein: 164
2nd International Stress Discussion Conference: 150
Scenedesmus: 165, 168, 194
Selye, Dr. Hans: 150-51, 152, 153
semiconductor: 180
Shibata, Dr. Mannen: 50
Smon's Disease: 102, 107
Sosa Texcoco S.A.: 9, 30, 32, 164, 166
Spirulina
    as energy booster: 4, 203, 204
    as world food: 6
    cost of: 7, 9
    growing of: 2-3, 7-8, 27, 36-38, 197-99
    harvesting of: 29, 30-32, 38, 53
    history of: 29-30
    safety of: 129-131, 133-137, 140-145
Spore, Prof.: 51
Stanley, Dr.: 153
steroids: 124, 125
stomach: 76, 77, 90, 116, 117, 119, 120, 179
stress: 115, 150-161
subcutaneous edema: 144
sugar: 60, 66, 81
Sugi, Dr. Yasusaburo Sugi: 19
Szent-Gyorgyi, Dr. Albert: 156

T

Takashima, Kasaku: 183
Takemoto, Prof. Kazuo: 56, 58
Takeuchi, Dr. Tadaya: 15, 55
Tanabe, Dr. Iwao: 123
Tanaka, Minoru: 89
Tohoku University: 50
Tokugawa Research Institute: 51
Tokyo Bureau of Health: 135
Tokyo College of Dentistry: 15
Tokyo Institute of Health: 135
Tokyo Stress Institute: 147
Tokyo Stress Research Society: 13-17
Tokyo University, Fisheries Dept.,
    College of Agriculture: 134
toxicity: 14-15, 56, 129-30
Toynbee, Arnold: 154, 158
trace elements: 23
tuberculosis: 58

U

Uematsu, Dr. Yoshio: 14, 139
ulcerated colitis: 114
ulcers: 76-77, 114, 120, 179
United Nations Industrial Development
    Organization: 9
United Nations Laboratories: 2
University Community School: 7
University of California: 180
University of Eastern Japan: 109
University of Northern Japan: 112
Uno, Makoto: 171
urine: 60, 61, 66, 103, 104
uveitis: 106

V

vitamins: 42, 70, 74, 75, 81, 86, 102,
    103, 154-56, 158, 159, 160, 202, 203,
    204-206

W

Walburg, Otto: 50
Watarai Clinic: 163
Watarai, Dr. Hiroshi: 163
weight: 120, 121, 137
world hunger: 6

Y

Yakult Corporation: 52
Yamada, Asst. Prof. Koji: 14, 133
Yamazaki, Yoshito, M.D.: 97
Yanagizawa, Dr. Fumimasa: 104
Yanagizawa Adult Disease Research
    Center: 104